Is Belief *Believable?*

"Among the virtues of this fine book are Christopher Kaczor's clarity of expression, ability to bring a personal touch to otherwise abstract philosophical arguments, and treatment of ideas that are important and historically influential but unjustly neglected in too much contemporary apologetics."

Edward Feser
Professor of Philosophy at Pasadena City College

"Christopher Kaczor again offers a compelling, multi-faceted exploration of a timeless concern: is belief rational? His answer deftly draws upon a wide range of sources—from classical philosophy to modern psychology—and, in so doing, offers a rich and accessible defense of faith."

Catherine Peters
Professor of Philosophy at Loyola Marymount University

"Christopher Kaczor provides a compelling account of why believing in God—and the God of the Bible, revealed in Jesus Christ—makes sense. He does so by uncovering much terrain, from philosophy, science, psychology, and even contemporary figures like Jordan Peterson. Kaczor is clear and insightful, especially when engaging the objections that afflict modern man's heart, such as the problem of evil and the apparent hiddenness of God. This book is sure to become a staple for those of faith and for those who are seeking—highly recommended!"

Andrew Swafford
Author of *Lunatic, Liar, or Lord: Unveiling the Truth of Catholicism with C.S. Lewis's Mere Christianity*

"Christopher Kaczor was one of the best students I have had at Boston College. Kaczor's book in defense of Christianity is simple and popular, not complex and technical, and deals with all the really important issues, arguments, and objections so fairly and reasonably and clearly that the reader has to pity the poor atheist."

Peter Kreeft
Professor of Philosophy at Boston College

Is Belief *Believable?*

Reasoning About God from Plato and Aquinas to C. S. Lewis and Jordan Peterson

Christopher Kaczor

Foreword by Bishop Robert Barron

Nihil Obstat: Reverend Monsignor Michael Heintz, PhD
Censor Librorum

Imprimatur: Most Reverend Kevin C. Rhoades
Bishop of Fort Wayne–South Bend
Given at Fort Wayne, Indiana, on April 29, 2025

Founded in 1865, Ave Maria Press is a ministry of the United States Province of Holy Cross.

www.avemariapress.com

Hardcover: ISBN-13 978-1-64680-427-6

E-book: ISBN-13 978-1-64680-428-3

Cover and text design by Andy Wagoner.

Printed and bound in the United States of America.

Library of Congress Cataloging-in-Publication Data is available.

For Sean and Christel Kelsey

Amicus Amicis

We shall soon be in a world in which a man may be howled down for saying that two and two make four, in which furious party cries will be raised against anybody who says that cows have horns, in which people will persecute the heresy of calling a triangle a three-sided figure, and hang a man for maddening a mob with the news that grass is green.

—G. K. Chesterton

Faith and reason are like two wings on which the human spirit rises to the contemplation of truth; and God has placed in the human heart a desire to know the truth—in a word, to know himself—so that, by knowing and loving God, men and women may also come to the fullness of truth about themselves.

—St. John Paul II

Contents

Foreword

Aristotle said, "All men by nature desire to know." We want to know not merely the trivialities of the moment, but what lasts and what matters most. This restless search for deeper insight is ultimately ordered to God. In *Is Belief Believable: Reasoning About God from Plato and Aquinas to C. S. Lewis and Jordan Peterson*, Christopher Kaczor helps us see the harmony of faith and reason in thinking about God and coming to know *who* God is.

Kaczor tackles key objections to belief in God such as skepticism, materialism, and scientism as well as the charge of Sigmund Freud that belief in the divine is merely wishful thinking. Kaczor then delves into the reasons offered by Plato, St. Augustine, Islamic thinkers, and St. Thomas Aquinas to believe that God exists.

What kind of God? Unlike many books that only explore God's existence, Kaczor presents, in terms understandable to the everyday reader, the natural theology of Aquinas on the divine mind, the divine will, and the divine love. Finally, this book turns to answer recent objections raised by the New Atheists to the God of the Bible.

Drawing on sources contemporary as well as classic, this book helps believers and skeptics alike think through the most important philosophical and spiritual questions of our day. Rather than a sterile struggle that pits the life of the mind against the life of the spirit, Kaczor proposes a reasonable faith and a faithful reason—the two wings, as St. John Paul II put it, that lift us to the divine.

Bishop Robert Barron
Founder of Word on Fire

Acknowledgments

This book was completed during a fellowship year at the de Nicola Center for Ethics and Culture at the University of Notre Dame. This Center was founded by David Solomon, who passed away during this year. David's legacy as a teacher, mentor, and friend endures in all of us who were his students and in the Center he founded. I am also grateful to Carter Snead, David's successor as Director of the Center, for granting me this fellowship year, and to Jennifer Newsome Martin, the current Director, for hosting me. Some chapters in this book appeared earlier as publications for Word on Fire, *Catholic World Report*, or *Catholic Answers Magazine*. I'm grateful for their permission to republish this work. I happily acknowledge Juan Granieri, Katherine Harvey, and Caroline Foreman for help in editing. Finally, I would also like to thank Josh Noem and the other great people at Ave Maria Press.

Christopher Kaczor
University of Notre Dame

Introduction

The First and the Last Thing Must Be Love

This book addresses challenges to belief in God and calls into question modern and postmodern obstacles to faith. St. Thomas Aquinas taught that there are two kinds of truths about God—truths that reason can show to be the case and truths that transcend what reason can show to be the case. While the first part of this book addresses preliminary obstacles to faith, the second part considers the truths of faith that reason can show to be true. St. Thomas Aquinas called these the *preambles of faith*. These are truths that are revealed by God but that can also be known through sound thinking. For example, using reason alone, we can come to realize that murder, stealing, and adultery are wrong. These are moral truths of natural law. But God also reveals that "you shall not murder," "you shall not steal," and "you shall not commit adultery" in the Ten Commandments (see Exodus 20). These moral truths are both able to be known through reason and able to be known through faith. Similarly, Thomas held that using reason we can know that God exists, that there is only one God, that God is intelligent, and other truths about the Divine. But, like the moral truths just mentioned, these truths about God are also revealed by God in the Bible. Not everyone has the time and intelligence to discover these truths, so God reveals them so that even little children can come to understand basic moral and theological truths. In our own times, C. S. Lewis and Jordan Peterson have done much work to make such insights accessible to general audiences.

On the other hand, St. Thomas Aquinas also taught that there are other truths about God that go beyond what reason can show to be the case. These are called *mysteries of faith*. If you met me, you could learn right away certain things about me just by using your reason. I'm not nine years old, and I'm not ninety years old. I don't weight five pounds, and I don't weight five hundred pounds. I'm not one foot tall, and I'm not ten feet tall. Reason alone can teach you a lot about me. If I met you, I could learn right away similar things about you. But you will have to reveal things about yourself to me if we are to really communicate and become friends. Who do you love? What do you fear? What are your dreams?

In the same way, we can know some things about God (especially about what God is not) by using our reason. But if we are going to really communicate with God and become friends with God, God must reveal things about himself to us. These truths that God reveals to us are the mysteries of faith. We cannot know through reason, through philosophical demonstration, that God is Father, Son, and Holy Spirit, that Jesus is fully divine and fully human, or that there are seven sacraments. Similarly, unless I reveal it to you, you cannot know the truth that just a moment ago I was thinking about my mom. But it is in fact true that I was thinking about her. So, St. Thomas holds that the mysteries of faith are true, that they are not *contrary* to reason, but that they transcend what reason operating alone can show to be true. This book focuses on the preambles of faith—those truths that can be known through reason—but the third part uses reason to remove some objections to the mysteries of faith. Again, in this endeavor, Lewis and Peterson are each in their own way helpful, but I will also draw on other contemporary resources to consider the questions at hand.

A fundamental theme of this book is that faith and reason are not opposed. Rather than think that we must choose either reason (philosophy, science, etc.) or faith (revelation, scripture, etc.), it turns out we can have a reasonable faith and a faithful reason. Faith and reason are not enemies, but friends.

Facing Family Feuds and Christmas Conflicts

But before turning to more distinctly intellectual matters, let's first consider some basics of good discussion. The topics covered in this book will provide you with a strong foundation for talking about faith and reason with others. However, when talking about these ideas with people you might fundamentally disagree with, it is important to remember that if people think that you hate them, they will not be open to listening to you and (potentially) learning from you, as well as (potentially) you learning from them. So, if you'd like to communicate effectively, it is best to *really listen* when others talk to you so that you know thoroughly and exactly what it is that they think. And what they think is just one part of the puzzle because also relevant is what they feel. If they feel you are an enemy, then they will be in debate mode, which makes it virtually impossible to have a fruitful conversation with them. What could be a fruitful conversation becomes something like the Democratic and Republican presidential candidates talking past one another, at best.

By contrast, good personal communication is an extension of good personal relationships. Rather than getting into debate mode, it is more helpful to adapt a mode of learning about the other person's perspective.

But I must confess I feel like the overweight doctor who is advising patients about how to lose weight. I don't always practice what I preach, and because of this I am worse off, and those around me are worse off. For example, on Christmas Day a few years ago, what could have been a time of warm reconnection of family members became a tense moment of sharp religious disagreement. Someone declared, "I think Jesus was married to Mary Magdalene and had kids with her." I could immediately feel the temperature of the room turn up to sauna-like levels.

What did I do? Well, not much, as a chorus of voices weighed in about a number of matters. And that was part of the problem. In real-life conversations, people ask multiple questions, make manifold assertions, and communicate much in verbal and body language. Such conversations feel like trying to return a serve in tennis when there are four people serving.

What I sometimes seek to do is return the serve, however many there are, with a powerful volley that cannot be answered and leaves everyone amazed. Point, set, match. But I believe that is the wrong approach in many, indeed most, situations. If you are onstage at the University of Notre Dame in a public debate with the atheist Richard Dawkins, it would be great to give an unanswerable reply. But what about after Christmas brunch in the company of family?

What could I have done in that moment that might have been better? I probably should have said, "I'd love to talk to you more about the idea that Jesus was married to Mary Magdalene and had kids with her. Right now, we are about to open presents, and I'd like to focus on that. But could we talk about this together after dinner tonight?" This response may have led to a more focused conversation that was not in debate mode in front of an audience.

When you get a chance to discuss issues of faith with people, it is good to ask questions. And by questions, I do not mean the kind of questions that Socrates asks in many Platonic dialogues. For these types of questions, there are usually only three proper answers, "Yes, Socrates," or "Most certainly, Socrates," and "Good point, Socrates."

Rather than ask rhetorical questions, we can ask real questions. For example, I could have asked, "Can you tell me more about the view that Jesus was married to Mary Magdalene? How did you arrive at this view? What would be the best reason to think this is true? And what would be the best reason to think this is not true?" Then, you can really listen to what they say, and respond with further questions about what they say to make 100 percent sure that you accurately understand their perspective. Your questions and follow-up questions can make clear that you are carefully listening and trying to understand as best you can what they mean. It is helpful to summarize what they said in your own words, compassionately and *not* sarcastically, to make certain you've understood them: "So, your view is that Jesus was married and had children because you read this in *The Da Vinci Code*. Is that right?" This active listening is an act of love. For when you love someone, you want to be united with them, and you are united with them when you really understand what they think and feel. If you do understand them, then your mind and their mind are in unity about what they believe and feel. Listening like a good friend is also important because only if you understand what their challenges, difficulties, questions, and concerns are can you engage with them as individuals.

You could imagine yourself as a doctor who is meeting a patient with complaints about various bodily ailments. "Doctor, I've been suffering from insomnia and stomach pain." A bad doctor might reply immediately on hearing a symptom or two, "Take this medication twice a day. It will take care of your symptoms." But a good doctor asks a whole series of questions aimed at diagnosing the actual ailment: "How long have you experienced these symptoms? What, if any, remedies have you tried? Let me gather more information about your blood pressure, temperature, and have some bloodwork done so that we can figure out how best to move forward." The best prescription in the world won't work if there is no match between the medication and the malady. The same is true in communicating about matters of faith. Make sure you know *exactly* what the issue is before recommending any particular answer. Often, the actual problem is emotional. Intellectual answers can remove intellectual difficulties, but the answer to emotional difficulties is not always intellectual.

So, although this book will say a lot about intellectual issues and various stumbling blocks as well as aids to faith, the most important thing that you can do to effectively share faith with others is to truly love them. This is especially true if they are alienated from faith. Let me close this introduction with a story of how this worked once in my life.

My father-in-law Dennis came out as gay and left the Catholic Church in 1971. As my wife Jennifer grew up, her relationship with her dad was rocky. They saw each other rarely because she lived on the West Coast, and he lived on the East Coast. When they did get together, sparks often flew. He would snap at her if she said or did anything that contradicted his own perspective.

But prickly personalities and religious differences need not destroy the love of a family. Jennifer took "honor thy father" not as a suggestion but as a commandment. So, she made enormous efforts to cultivate a good relationship with her father. Every time Jen spoke with him on the phone, her face was braced for trouble, her voice tensed up, and her every word was picked with the deliberation of a diplomat. Since he lived in New York and we lived in Los Angeles, we didn't see him often.

However, that changed when we moved for a fellowship year to Princeton. We would travel to New York City every three weeks or so to visit with Dennis and his legal husband, Claudio. We kept it light and focused on common interests. We never talked about religion unless they brought it up. We knew where they stood, and they knew where we stood. As the year went on, Dennis became more and more ill. It became clear that death would visit him soon.

On our final visit to New York City, we all knew that this would be the last time that we would ever see each other. Jen and I were heading from Princeton back to Los Angeles, and Dennis was moving to Claudio's home country of Uruguay. They gave us a few mementos to pack in our car, and they walked us out to the sidewalk to see us off.

When I said goodbye to Claudio, he told me, "You know, Chris, I was terrified to meet you. I'm an atheist, a Jew, and gay. So, I thought you would hate me. But you have never been anything but loving and kind to me." On his cheek, I gave Dennis a kiss goodbye. Tears filled my eyes as Jennifer and her dad embraced in their final farewell.

So, Dennis and Claudio moved to Uruguay, and Jennifer and I moved back to Los Angeles. But Jennifer kept in regular contact with her dad on the phone. A nurse who cared for him gave us updates. Within months of the move, the nurse told us his death would be within days.

I asked Jen, “Should we try to see if your dad would allow a priest to give him last rites?” She said she would see if he was open to it. She called and talked to him. But Dennis didn’t think he was dying, so there was no need at all, he thought, for last rites.

Well, would he be open to a priest coming to pray with him, to give him the Anointing of the Sick? Yes, he’d do that.

I reached out to a priest friend in Los Angeles, Fr. Paul Donlan, who connected me to another priest living in Uruguay. This priest rushed over for a visit to my father-in-law. The priest heard Dennis’s confession (his first in fifty years), administered last rites, and gave him viaticum, his final Holy Communion. In the last picture we have of Dennis, just days before he died, he looks totally exhausted. In his emaciated hand, he holds a crucifix the priest had given him. The nurse told my wife that he wouldn’t let go of it. She washed his hands around the crucifix.

As we will see in this book, the essence of God is love. My father-in-law returned to the sacraments, not because my wife defeated him in argument, but because she did her best to be a loving daughter. She loved him in her deeds; she loved him in her words. An important way to love someone is to speak about what we understand the truth to be, including our best understanding of the truth about the highest things. Whether we are seeking to understand God better ourselves or trying to talk with others about God, we must always conduct these studies and conversations in the spirit of love. This is the only way to truly understand what God is like.

With this in mind, we will now begin to explore some of the most important questions in life—namely, does God exist, and, if so, what is he like? Each chapter will examine a question about

God, and the conclusion we draw will tell us something new about his existence or nature. The chapters in this book build on each other like rungs on a ladder. We will begin by looking at the foundational principle of all reasoning, and with this principle we will analyze common counterarguments to God's existence. With those obstacles removed, we will then examine the philosophical reasons to believe in the existence of a being like God. And finally, we will consider obstacles to belief in the God of the Bible.

Obstacles to Belief in God

1

Where to Begin?

What Aristotle and Avicenna Can Teach Us About First Principles

In this book, we are considering obstacles to belief in God, reasons to believe in God, and belief in the God of the Bible. In all these discussions, we need a place from which to begin. We need first principles, or basic beliefs, in order to have any conversation. So, in this chapter, we look at the most basic of all beliefs: *the principle of noncontradiction*. Even if you have never heard of the principle of noncontradiction, you have in fact used this principle. This first principle is a bit like gravity. A person may not know the word *gravity* or may never have attended a lecture in physics, but still lives and acts in accordance with gravity. So too, the principle of noncontradiction is known by children, even though children have not yet studied philosophy. This chapter makes explicit what everyone already knows, but may not know that they know.

In one of Edward St. Aubyn's novels, a man is asked if he is his own worst enemy. "I certainly hope so," the man replies. "I dread to think what would happen if somebody else turned out to be better at it than me."[1] In the life of the mind, one way to be your own worst enemy is by means of self-defeating statements, such as, "I am not writing in English right now" or "I never, never, never use the word *never*"—statements that cannot possibly be true because the claim being made is undermined by the claim being made. A statement that is self-defeating is like a mixed martial arts fighter who knocks himself out (yes, this happens).

Timothy Keller, author of *The Reason for God*, provides other examples of self-defeating statements: "Everyone in the world is an evangelist. Even telling someone they can't proselytize is a form of proselytizing your views."[2] He notes, "Everyone makes exclusive truth claims. You may say 'no religion should say their view of reality is superior to everyone else's' but at that moment you are claiming that your view of reality is superior—more worthy of acceptance—than theirs."[3] Keller also points out that "to insist doctrine doesn't matter is really a doctrine itself" and "How could you possibly know that no religion can see the whole truth unless you yourself have the superior, comprehensive knowledge of spiritual reality you just claimed none of the religions have?"[4]

Pointing to self-defeating statements may seem like a verbal trick. But the self-defeating nature of such claims is grounded not in trickery but in reality. What reality? Aristotle pointed out that all thinking, all speaking, and all doing rely on the bedrock reality of the principle of noncontradiction—namely, that "a thing cannot be and not be at the same time and in the same respect."[5] Even children playing hide-and-seek implicitly use this principle. They know that their friend cannot both be and not be hiding in the pantry.

Of course, some people do deny the principle of noncontradiction. In such cases, the medieval Islamic philosopher Avicenna suggested tough medicine, "Anyone who denies the law of non-contradiction should be beaten and burned until he admits that to be beaten is not the same as not to be beaten, and to be burned is not the same as not to be burned."[6] A more gentle approach is to point out that all people (including those who deny the principle) rely on the principle of noncontradiction every day whenever they think something, say something, or do something. They are thinking rather than not thinking, speaking rather than not speaking, doing rather than not doing. Even to deny the principle of noncontradiction is to unwittingly rely on the principle of noncontradiction. To deny any statement is to recognize a difference between denying that statement and affirming that statement, which is to make use of the principle of noncontradiction.

Given the principle of noncontradiction, a statement cannot both be true and not true at the same time and in the same respect. If it were true that each and every sentence I write is exactly three words long, then this sentence would also be exactly three words long, but it isn't.

Scientists are not immune from expressing self-defeating statements. For example, Richard Dawkins writes, "Truth is real and science is the best way we have of finding it. 'Alternative ways of knowing' may be consoling, they may be sincere, they may be quaint, they may have a poetic or mythic beauty, but the one thing they are not is true."[7] Science does indeed help us discover various truths, and it is indeed the best way to discover particular kinds of truth, like what medications are best for asthma treatment. But it does not follow from these claims that other ways of knowing—philosophy, for example—are not true. The claim that "alternative ways of knowing are not true" is *not* itself a claim of science, so any attempted justification must be based on alternative ways of knowing. The fundamental claim of scientism that "science and science alone provides the truth" is not proven scientifically. There is no experiment in physics or biology or chemistry or any other science that shows that science alone is true. So Dawkins must rely on "other ways of knowing" in his denial that "other ways of knowing" can come to the truth.

The philosopher Ludwig Wittgenstein wrote, "Even if *all possible* scientific questions be answered, the problems of life have still not been touched at all."[8] Should I marry this person? Should I have a child? How should I spend my limited time, treasure, and talent? Some of the most important questions in life are questions that science simply cannot answer. Among the most important questions we can ask are questions about God.

The late, great film critic Roger Ebert wrote, "I no longer lost any sleep over the questions of God and infinity. I understood they could have no answers."[9] But, of course, to assert that questions about God have no answers is itself an answer. The person who responds to the question, "What can be known about God?" with "nothing at all" is offering no less an answer than the answer of St. Thomas Aquinas. He believed that using reason alone we can know of the existence of one God who is intelligent, good, and loving.

Self-defeating statements are even found among philosophers. In his 1748 book *An Enquiry Concerning Human Understanding*, David Hume provided a good example in what is called Hume's fork:

> If we take in our hand any volume; of divinity or school metaphysics, for instance; let us ask, Does it contain any abstract reasoning concerning quantity or number? No. Does it contain any experimental reasoning concerning matters of fact and existence? No. Commit it then to the flames: for it can contain nothing but sophistry and illusion.[10]

But note, does this quotation from Hume contain any abstract reasoning concerning quantity or number? No. Does it contain any experimental reasoning concerning matters of fact and existence? No. Then, according to Hume's own principles, we should commit his writing to the flames, for it can contain nothing but sophistry and illusion. With his fork, Hume stabs himself.

In 1936, a twenty-four-year-old philosopher named A. J. Ayer developed Hume's view in his book *Language, Truth, and Logic*. In what is called logical positivism, Ayer taught that no proposition is meaningful if it is neither a tautology (e.g., "A bachelor is an unmarried man") nor empirically verifiable (by scientific experiments, at least in principle). But the claim "No proposition is meaningful if it is neither a tautology nor empirically verifiable" is itself neither a tautology nor empirically verifiable. So, logical positivism, according to its own standards, is meaningless.

In 1976, Bryan Magee asked Ayer, "Logical positivism must have had real defects. What do you now, in retrospect, think the main ones were?" Ayer replied, "Well, I suppose the most important of the defects was that nearly all of it was false."[11]

Who says philosophy never makes progress? And now, armed with the principle of noncontradiction, we will begin our investigation into what can be known about God through reason.

2

Can We Know Anything About God?

Responding to Immanuel Kant

Immanuel Kant is one of the most important philosophers who ever lived. Kant did *believe* in God, yet he was skeptical of the ability of human reason to know anything about the Transcendent, including whether God exists. Why did Kant hold this view?

In his notoriously difficult book *Critique of Pure Reason*, Kant drew a distinction between the reality of things in themselves (*noumena*) and things as they appear to us (*phenomena*). He argued that we do not have access to the *noumena*, only to the *phenomena*. Our concepts apply to the *appearances* of the world, since they are derived solely from these appearances. But we cannot know the *reality* of things in themselves, so our concepts cannot give us knowledge of that reality.

How does God fit into this distinction between appearance and reality? If our concepts don't help us to know the reality of things in themselves, then our concepts cannot help us to know the reality of God in himself. God does not appear in the world like an elephant explored by blind men. Our concepts *can* properly apply to the appearance of the elephant, which we can see, touch, and smell. But our concepts cannot apply to what does not appear to our senses, such as God. Thus, if Kant is right about how our concepts relate to appearance and reality, our concepts cannot give us any knowledge of God. The great University of Notre Dame philosopher Alvin Plantinga summarizes Kant's point as follows: "God, who is reality *in excelsis*, is so far above us, or beyond us, that our puny minds can't reach him at all. Our minds, and our thought, our language simply have no purchase on God."[1] So, since our arguments and thoughts use only human concepts, it is impossible not only to argue for the existence of God but also for us to know anything whatsoever about God.

But Plantinga points out the problem with this view: "The statement that we can't think about God—the *statement* that God is such that we can't think about him—is obviously a statement about God; if we cannot think about God, then we can't say about him that we can't think of him."[2] In other words, to say, "I can say nothing about God" is in fact to say *something* about God; so, "I can say nothing about God" is a self-defeating statement. Plantinga continues, "Perhaps there are things we can't think about, maybe things in some other part of the universe. If so, we can't pick out any of those things and say of it that we can't think about it."[3] So, this Kantian argument provides no good reason for believing that we cannot think about God.

Another problem arises. Either our concepts *do* help us know the reality of things in themselves or they don't. But if we really cannot form concepts to think or talk accurately about the reality of things in themselves, then we cannot in fact know the distinction between the reality of things in themselves and the appearances of the world to us. The reality-appearance distinction transcends mere appearance. If our concepts don't give us understanding of the reality of things in themselves, we cannot use these concepts to draw the distinction between the reality of things in themselves and the appearances of the world to us. So, the Kantian distinction is self-defeating, undermining itself. As Kant's great critic Hegel pointed out, "The very fact that something is determined as a limitation implies that the limitation is already transcended."[4] In his *Tractatus*, Ludwig Wittgenstein expressed a similar thought: "In order to draw a limit to thinking we should have to be able to think both sides of this limit (we should therefore have to be able to think what cannot be thought)."[5]

In other words, the concept of a distinction between the reality of things in themselves and the appearances of the world to us is not itself an appearance of the world to us. So, if our concepts apply *only* to the appearances of the world, then we cannot have a concept of this distinction. But we do have this concept. So, we can have concepts about what goes beyond the appearances of things. The fact that God doesn't appear to us like another object in the world is no reason to think we cannot use our concepts to think or speak accurately about God.

Jim McCrea makes a similar point:

> To deny we can know things in themselves is a denial that we can know being—but to deny we can know being, means that we have a concept of being to deny—we cannot deny something we have no concept of—for example, to say there is no dog in the room means that we must have an idea of what a dog is to meaningfully deny that it is in the room—similarly, we must have a concept of being to deny we can know being—however, a concept of being can only come from being—this is because what is other than being is non-being, and non-being cannot mediate a knowledge of being because it is not real.[6]

So, the Kantian critique that we cannot know anything about God—including whether he exists—does not work.

How would St. Thomas Aquinas respond to the claim that human concepts cannot be used about God? Thomas agrees that our human concepts and language about God cannot capture the divine essence. For this reason, Thomas thought that the best way to move toward a greater understanding of God was by removing misunderstandings of God. This is called *remotion* or *apophatic theology* or *negative theology.* The most accurate speech about God is by means of denial of what God is not. God is not finite. God is not a body. God is not created.

However, while it is true that our finite minds cannot perfectly comprehend an infinite God, that does not mean that we cannot know anything at all about God. We can come to know something (not everything) about Michelangelo by examining his fresco *The Last Judgment*. We can know something (not everything) about Emily Dickinson by studying her poem "Because I could not stop for Death—he kindly stopped for me." So, too, we can come to know something (not everything) about the Creator by examining the creation. Since God's creation tells us something about God, we can use words derived from God's creation to tell us something about God.

Some people say, "It is impossible to do metaphysics after Kant." But I say, it is impossible to take Kant's critique of metaphysics for granted after Plantinga.

3

Are All Things God?

Against the Monism of Shankara and Parmenides

You may have heard of the idea that "all is one" or "we are all God" or "God is you, me, the tree, the rock, and all existence." This view that all reality is one, that the distinctions between things are mere illusions, is sometimes called *monism*. In the East, the Hindu philosopher Shankara advocated this view. In the West, the Greek philosopher Parmenides held that reality is one unchanging Being. If "all is one," multiplicity is a deceptive appearance. Should we accept this idea that all reality is really just one?

If our senses are even minimally accurate, it is clear that all reality is *not* one. When the lion eats the lamb, the lion is nourished and the lamb is destroyed. When your hand is burned by the stove, two different realities interact. So, one of the costs of monism is the rejection of all the information that we gather from our senses.

Virtually no one consistently rejects all the information that comes from the senses. In eating, we distinguish the fresh-off-the-grill cheeseburger from the shards of broken glass found in a dirty dumpster. When we walk, we avoid heading into traffic or off steep cliffs. So, adopting monism produces a fundamental inconsistency between theory and practice. Monism drives a Mack truck between one's philosophy of life and one's living of life. Anyone who lives as if "all reality is one" does not live long.

Another cost of the belief that all reality is one is the denial of change. Let's say you rise from a chair and walk across the room to get a glass of water. That change in bodily location is only possible if there is in fact a *difference* between your current location and your future location. But if all reality is really one, then this difference in location is just an illusion, so you cannot change location. This is hard to believe.

Change involves an actualization of a potency. When you change location, you move from actually being in one place toward where you potentially could be. When you get a tan, your skin goes from actually being one shade to realizing its potency to be a darker shade. But if all reality is one, then there is no difference between actuality and potentiality. That means no change is possible.

But if no change is possible, then it is also impossible to change your mind. Yet even if our senses are deceiving us and the changes we perceive in the material world are an illusion, we still have repeatedly and directly experienced changes in our mind. Indeed, we can have such an experience right now. Three pink elephants play soccer on a green lawn in front of the Eiffel Tower. I'm guessing before you read the previous sentence, you were not thinking about pink elephants or green lawns or the Eiffel Tower. Your mind changed from not thinking about these things to thinking about these things. So, even if our senses were completely deceiving us, change actually takes place in our minds.

But if change takes place, then the view that "all things are one" is false. If all things really were one, and all distinctions merely an illusion, then we could never change our minds from potentially thinking about elephants to actually thinking about elephants.

Here's yet another problem with monism. Advocates for monism hold that it is true that "all things are one" and that it is false that there are in fact many different things. But this assertion presupposes a difference between truth and falsity. So, the claim that "all things are one" is a self-defeating statement.

Moreover, advocates for monism hold it is better to believe their view than views they reject. But this preference for accepting their own views presupposes that their views are not the same as the views they reject. So, their own view implicitly affirms that difference *is* real, that reality is *not* all one. Monism ends up defeating itself because it involves self-contradiction. So, all things are not one. God is not all things.

Yet St. Thomas Aquinas taught that God is *in* all things by his essence, presence, and power. What does this mean? It does not mean monism. God is not in all things like ice is in an ice sculpture or like water is in a water balloon. Rather, God is in all things a bit like William Shakespeare is in all his plays. Shakespeare wrote into existence Lady Macbeth, King Lear, Juliet Capulet, and Prince Hamlet. Shakespeare placed them in the time and the place of his choosing. He understood these characters because he was the cause of each of them.

Of course, we are not like characters in a play who must say and do whatever the playwright has written. We have free will. Indeed, it is our freedom that leads to our tragedies, comedies, and histories. Shakespeare saw our world as a great drama: "All the world's a stage, And all the men and women merely players."[1] He believed this drama has a Director who works with our freedom: "There's a divinity that shapes our ends, rough-hew them how we will."[2]

Justin Brierley expresses this view in his fine book *The Surprising Rebirth of Belief in God: Why the New Atheism Grew Old and Secular Thinkers are Considering Christianity Again*. Brierley writes that the story of Christ is:

> a grand story that declares that every individual story matters. Far from being one more product of a mindless, purposeless universe headed towards oblivion, we have each been offered an integral role in a cosmic drama. What you do with your part is up to you, but you are nevertheless invited into a story that is being woven through time and space, a story in which you are intended, purposed, and loved.[3]

There are characters in search of their Author, as Ralph McInerny said. There are characters who flee him down the nights and down the days, as the poet Francis Thompson wrote. What matters most is that the Author always seeks us. But that Author is neither the characters nor the stage. All is not one.

4

Does Science Disprove God?

The Incompatibility of Science and Materialism

If the distinctions we see in the world are real, other questions arise about reality. Is all reality nothing but a collection of atoms? Materialism can be defined as the worldview that nothing exists except what is material and physical. As Julian Baggini explains in his book *Atheism: A Very Short Introduction*, "There is one kind of stuff in the universe and it is physical, out of this stuff comes minds, beauty, emotions, moral values—in short the full gamut of phenomena that gives richness to human life."[1] If materialism is true, there is no God, no soul, and no afterlife.

The chief argument *for* materialism is the success of science. Science proceeds by assuming materialism is true, and science clearly shows us truths about reality. Given the spectacular success of science in curing diseases and providing technological advances, it is therefore unscientific and irrational not to accept materialism.

This argument fails to distinguish between methodological materialism and ontological materialism. Methodological materialism is conducting scientific experiments by *focusing* simply on what is material, what can be quantified and measured. Ontological materialism, on the other hand, is *believing* that only matter exists. Materialism as a practice of science is distinct from materialism as a philosophy of reality.

Throughout history, many successful scientists (Copernicus, Newton, Kepler, Mendel, Lemaître, Einstein, Collins, Huberman) have believed that God exists. They have accepted methodological materialism in practicing science but have *rejected* the philosophy of materialism. Are these scientists inconsistent? Not in the least. In doing math, we factor out as irrelevant whether the problem is written in black ink or white chalk. But black ink and white chalk do *exist* and are *relevant* in other ways. So, too, science factors out nonmaterial causes in conducting experiments. But it does not therefore follow that *only* material causes exist. As Edward Feser has pointed out, the success of metal detectors in finding metal does not show that metal alone exists. So, too, the success of science in understanding matter does not show that matter alone exists.

Indeed, the claim that only material realities exist is difficult to reconcile with the reality that 2 + 2 = 4. This reality is not material. Of course, every written representation of the reality that 2 + 2 = 4 has certain material characteristics. But the written *representation* and the *reality* are two different things. I can write "2 + 2 = 4" in large script or small, in pink ink or in crimson crayon, but none of these changes in written *representation* change the *reality* of 2 + 2 = 4 in the least. These written representations manifest the same unaltered reality, despite the changing and changeable molecules of representation. The innumerable truths of mathematics are not material realities with a particular length or color or weight or chemical composition. Before the material universe came into existence 13.8 billion years ago, it was the case that 2 + 2 = 4, and it would remain the case even if the material universe ceased to exist. So, since there are realities that are not material, materialism as a worldview is false.

Chemistry, biology, and physics all presuppose the truth of mathematics. For example, Newton's second law of motion, "Force equals mass times acceleration," assumes the truth of multiplication, as does $E = mc^2$. But if the philosophy of materialism were true, immaterial realities would not explain reality. Immaterial mathematical claims would turn out to be just concepts in our minds, mere fictions, stories we make up that don't correspond to what actually is outside our minds. If mathematical truths don't really exist, then the application of mathematical formulas would not help us to understand the world. If math is mere fiction, we might as well use *Jack and the Beanstalk* to explain the biology of plant growth, *Beauty and the Beast* to understand endangered species, or *Aladdin and His Magic Lamp* to engineer planes. But science does help explain reality, so math is not fiction. Scientific success is not possible without reliance on the truth of immaterial mathematical realities. Indeed, scientific success points to the truths of mathematics, and the truths of mathematics are not material realities.

The philosophy of materialism and practice of science are difficult to reconcile in another way. If materialism as a philosophy is right, then the *only* realities that exist are composed of chemicals, molecules, and atoms. But ethical norms are not material realities. The ethical propositions "Seek the truth," "Don't falsify lab results," and "Don't fabricate your work" are not composed of chemicals, molecules, and atoms (though their written manifestations are). Despite the efforts of some philosopher advocates of materialism, the "is" of matter alone doesn't readily yield the "ought" of ethics. Science is a collaborative endeavor that cannot succeed if scientists falsify their lab results and fabricate their findings. So unless scientists live in accordance with these nonmaterial realities, then science as a social practice cannot flourish.

What is the bottom line? The success of science does not justify materialism as a worldview. Copernicus, Newton, Kepler, Mendel, Lemaître, Einstein, Collins, Huberman, and a majority of Nobel Prize winners in science in the twentieth century believed in the existence of God (so they rejected materialism as a worldview), but they did excellent science. Indeed, the success of science is a reason to reject the philosophy of materialism. Science presupposes the reality of nonphysical mathematical truths. The practice of science also requires acting in ways consistent with nonmaterial realities of moral norms such as “Seek the truth,” “Don’t falsify lab results,” and “Don’t fabricate your work.” So, combining the philosophy of materialism and science is self-defeating. To be consistent, we must choose science *or* materialism.

5

Is God Too Good to Be True?

Jordan Peterson, C. S. Lewis, and the "Wishful Thinking" Objection

The religious views of the public intellectual Jordan Peterson are a moving target as his thought continues to develop and he seeks greater insight. But in his first best-selling book, *12 Rules for Life*, Peterson writes, "I had outgrown the shallow Christianity of my youth by the time I could understand the fundamentals of Darwinian theory. After that, I could not distinguish the basic elements of Christian belief from wishful thinking."[1] In a podcast after *12 Rules for Life*, he expresses a similar worry: "There seems to be something too convenient about C. S. Lewis, his insistence that [the perfection of Christ] also had to manifest itself concretely in reality at one point in history."[2]

Is Christian belief a case of wishful thinking? Is it too good to be true, a convenient creed that should be rejected because it is *too* convenient?

C. S. Lewis provides some insights relevant for these questions: "I didn't go to religion to make me 'happy.' I always knew a bottle of Port could do that. If you want a religion to make you feel really comfortable, I certainly don't recommend Christianity."[3] Despite its convenience, Lewis rejected a watered-down Christianity, "the view which simply says there is a good God in Heaven and everything is all right—leaving out all the difficult and terrible doctrines about sin and hell and the devil, and the redemption."[4]

Lewis accepted these inconvenient teachings because Jesus taught them (Mt 25, Mk 9:43, Lk 16, Jn 5:29). If Lewis sought a merely consoling creed, it would have been like H. Richard Niebuhr's account of watered-down Christianity: "A God without wrath brought men without sin into a Kingdom without judgment through the ministrations of a Christ without a Cross."[5]

Peterson is certainly right that Christianity is in some respects comforting and convenient. For example, how consoling it is to believe that God's mercy is greater than any human sin. Yet this, in itself, does not show that Christianity is wishful thinking. As Lewis points out:

> Suppose I think, after doing my accounts, that I have a large balance at the bank. And suppose you want to find out whether this belief of mine is 'wishful thinking.' You can never come to any conclusion by examining my psychological condition. Your only chance of finding out is to sit down and work through the sum yourself. When you have checked my figures, then, and then only, will you know whether I have that balance or not. If you find my arithmetic correct, then no amount of vapouring about my psychological condition can be anything but a waste of time. If you find my arithmetic wrong, then it may be relevant to explain psychologically how I came to be so bad at my arithmetic, and the doctrine of the concealed wish will become relevant—but only *after* you have yourself done the sum and discovered me to be wrong on purely arithmetical grounds. It is the same with all thinking and all systems of thought.[6]

Human thinkers give rise to systems of thought, and wishful thinkers are found on all sides of religious questions. For example, the atheist Thomas Nagel wrote: "I want atheism to be true and am made uneasy by the fact that some of the most intelligent and well-informed people I know are religious believers. It isn't just that I don't believe in God and, naturally, hope that I'm right in my belief. It's that I hope there is no God! I don't want there to be a God; I don't want the universe to be like that."[7] We cannot validly reason from Nagel's atheistic wish to a conclusion that therefore God must exist. So too, we cannot reason from the fact that the Christian wishes that God raised Jesus from the dead to the conclusion that therefore the Resurrection didn't happen.

Wishful thinking may also be found in considerations of what God is like. Lewis wrote: "The Life-Force is a sort of tame God. You can switch it on when you want, but it will not bother you. All the thrills of religion and none of the cost. Is the Life-Force the greatest achievement of wishful thinking the world has yet seen?"[8] By contrast, in some rooms, "the temperature drops as soon as you mention a God who has purposes and performs particular actions, who does one thing and not another, a concrete, choosing, commanding, prohibiting God with a determinate character."[9]

As Lewis put it in his book *Miracles*, "An 'impersonal God'—well and good. A subjective God of beauty, truth and goodness, inside our own heads—better still. A formless life-force surging through us, a vast power which we can tap—best of all. But God Himself, alive, pulling at the other end of the cord, perhaps approaching at an infinite speed, the hunter, king, husband—that is quite another matter."[10]

But Lewis would be the first to point out that we cannot logically conclude from the wishes of people for a tame Life-Force God that these wishes (somehow) show that the personal, law-giving God of the Bible exists. Regardless of the wishes of the atheist, or the theist, or the agnostic, in fact either this God really does exist or he does not.

Lewis offers considerations relevant for all who share Peterson's concerns about Christianity being too good to be true: "If Christianity is untrue, then no honest man will want to believe it, however helpful it might be: if it is true, every honest man will want to believe it, even if it gives him no help at all."[11]

6

Is Religion the Opium of the People?

Sigmund Freud, Karl Marx, and the Genetic Fallacy

Sigmund Freud and Karl Marx adopted similar strategies to discredit belief in God. Freud held that belief in God arose from an unconscious childish wish for protection from a heavenly father figure: "At bottom God is nothing more than an exalted father."[1] Marx held that belief in God arose from economic alienation: "Religion is the sigh of the oppressed creature, the heart of a heartless world and the soul of soulless conditions. It is the opium of the people."[2] According to Freud and Marx, belief in God arose from wish fulfillment or exploitation, and so, it might be concluded, God does not exist.

Both of these critiques are logically fallacious. In his book *Socratic Logic*, Peter Kreeft points out that the *genetic fallacy*:

> consists in "refuting" an idea by showing some suspicious psychological origin of it. . . . No matter how egregious the psychological origins of a belief may be, the logic of the argument for it is independent of the psychology. If Einstein had been a vicious Nazi and had discovered the Theory of Relativity only in order to give Hitler the atom bomb to kill his enemies and conquer the world, that would not prove that E does not equal MC^2.[3]

In fact, important scientific discoveries have had unlikely origins. The inventor of the periodic table, Dmitri Mendeleev, discovered the relationship between chemical elements and atomic weight through a vivid dream. The chemist August Kekulé gained insight into the structure of atoms in benzene when he dreamed of a snake eating its own tail. The microbiologist Alexander Fleming discovered that penicillin destroys bacteria because he didn't properly clean his lab. The *genesis* of an idea does not determine the *truth* of an idea. So, even if Freud and Marx were right about the psychological origins of belief in God, that would not show that God does not exist.

But were Freud and Marx right? Discovering the psychological origins of beliefs can be tricky. Did I come to believe house painting is a noble profession because of a traumatic experience in first grade while finger painting with Peter, an unrecognized fear of my father-in-law Miles, or a misplaced jealousy of my college roommate Chad? If I visit a psychologist for years, I may still never know for sure.

But, supposedly, according to Freud and Marx, in all times and in all cultures everyone in the world who believes in God has exactly the same psychological motivation. Given the vast diversity of the human experience, this is hard to believe. Even psychologists are amateurs about people they have never personally evaluated. As Justice Antonin Scalia pointed out, "Interior decorating is a rock-hard science compared to psychology practiced by amateurs."[4]

But suppose, for the sake of argument, that we could somehow know that everyone in the world, in every century and in every culture, who believes in God in fact does have exactly the same psychological motivation. This would still not show that God does not exist. After all, God could design us so that common psychological motivations lead human beings to believe that God exists.

On the other hand, maybe distorted psychological motivations explain *not* believing in God. In his book *Faith of the Fatherless: The Psychology of Atheism*, NYU Professor Emeritus of Psychology

Paul Vitz offers biographical surveys of the lives of famous atheists, including Marx, Freud, Sartre, Nietzsche, Hitchens, Dawkins, and Dennett. Vitz discovered a common pattern. All of these famous atheists had dead, absent, or abusive fathers. Vitz writes, "Therefore, in the Freudian framework, atheism is an illusion caused by the oedipal desire to kill the father (God) and replace him with oneself."[5]

But even if it were true that all atheists share the same experience of defective fathers (all of them?), that too would provide no evidence that God does exist. Vitz's psychological genealogy of atheism as arising from defective father syndrome may be true, but it does not prove that atheism is false. The genetic fallacy is a fallacy whether used for or against atheism.

In his essay "Bulverism," C. S. Lewis points out still further problems with trying to discredit beliefs by pointing to their (alleged) psychological genesis: "The first is, are *all* thoughts thus tainted at the source, or only some? The second is, does the taint invalidate the tainted thought—in the sense of making it untrue—or not? If they say that *all thoughts* are thus tainted, then, of course, we must remind them that Freudianism and Marxism are as much systems of thought as Christian theology or philosophical idealism. The Freudian and Marxian are in the same boat with all the rest of us, and cannot criticize us from outside. They have sawn off the branch they were sitting on."[6] If all thoughts are mere rationalizations of erotic desires, then so is the thought that "all thoughts are mere rationalizations of erotic desires." If all claims are unjustified epiphenomena generated by an economic superstructure, then also unjustified is the claim that "all claims are unjustified epiphenomenal rationalizations generated by an economic superstructure." Such thoughts and claims are self-defeating.

Lewis continues: "If, on the other hand, they say that the taint need not invalidate their thinking, then neither need it invalidate ours. In which case they have saved their own branch, but also saved ours along with it."[7] If Freud can make statements that are true, despite the irrational workings of his subconscious, then so can the critic of Freud. If Marx can have thoughts that correspond to reality, despite economic circumstances, then so can the critic of Marx. In vain, then, do we try to discredit an idea on the basis of its alleged origin as a rationalization of erotic or economic interests.

Finally, the genetic fallacy leads to lazy thinking. Rather than actually engaging with what a person says, assessing the reasons for or against the belief in question, the lazy thinker can dismiss any belief by discrediting its messenger. As Thomas Sowell observed, "It is amazing how many people think that they can answer an argument by attributing bad motives to those who disagree with them. Using this kind of reasoning, you can believe or not believe anything about anything, without having to bother to deal with facts or logic."[8] A mind is a terrible thing to waste on logical fallacies.

7

Can Psychology Explain Away God?

Three Psychological Approaches to Religion

Psychology as a discipline of study has no single view about religion. Approaches range from hostile opposition to enthusiastic appropriation. The first significant approach we will consider develops Sigmund Freud's antipathy to religion and is represented today by figures such as Steven Pinker.[1] These atheist psychologists attempt to explain away religious beliefs as either mere by-products of evolution (spandrels) or evolutionary adaptations such as providing comfort in suffering or bringing the community together to enhance survival. These psychologists seem to think that explaining the *origin* of a belief also undermines the *truth* of the belief. If religion developed through evolutionary means, they argue, then religion must be false.

This view is, as noted in the previous chapter, a version of the genetic fallacy. But another trouble with such dismissals of religious beliefs and practices is that they often do not actually explain the beliefs in question. For instance, some people hold that the Catholic teaching on contraception is merely aimed at producing as many babies born to Catholics as possible. But if so, then why would the Church also teach many things that do not maximize procreation such as celibacy for priests and nuns, monogamy rather than polygamy, a prohibition on adultery (which would in some cases lead to pregnancy), and an allowance of natural family planning for purposes of avoiding pregnancy? If religion is aimed at bringing about comfort, then why do Christians have beliefs that are not comforting, like hell? If religious belief and practice is simply a means of survival, then why celebrate martyrs who died rather than deny the faith?

A similar, although more positive, approach to the relationship of psychology and religion is represented by the thought of Martin Seligman. He notes:

> For half a century after Freud's disparagements, social science remained dubious about religion. . . . About twenty years ago, however, the data on the positive psychological effects of faith started to provide a countervailing force. Religious Americans are clearly less likely to abuse drugs, commit crimes, divorce, and kill themselves. They are also physically healthier and live longer. Religious mothers of children with disabilities fight depression better, and religious people are less thrown by divorce, unemployment, illness, and death. More directly relevant is the fact that survey data consistently show religious people as being somewhat happier and more satisfied with life than non-religious people.[2]

Indeed, religious practice normally enhances positive emotion, engagement with activities, relationships with others, meaning-making, and achievement in a number of ways.[3] Contemporary psychological research provides decisive evidence against the old canard that religious faith and practice damages mental health. Rather than repressing sexuality, married couples who practice a faith together are more likely than nonreligious people to report satisfying sex lives.[4] Although Seligman sees the psychological and social utility of practicing faith, he is still skeptical of God's existence (at least God as traditionally understood).[5] Seligman views religious practice as (on the whole) healthy and beneficial for human well-being, and yet in his efforts as an amateur theologian and philosopher he also views traditional religious belief as irrational and unjustified.

In addition to the Jungian approach of Jordan Peterson, a third significant approach to psychology and religion is found in the work of psychologists such as Paul Vitz, who is a practicing Catholic.[6] This approach manifests an intentional integration of psychology and Catholic Christianity, similar in some ways to St. Augustine's integration of the pagan philosopher Plato with biblical Christianity. This approach involves appropriating what is legitimate and useful from secular psychology but modifying or rejecting what is contrary to true faith and practice. Careful discernment is needed to distinguish what is true from what is false, what is useful from what is counterproductive for the person of faith. Yet, because God is the ultimate author of both the truths of faith and the truths of reason as found in the created order (including in the minds of human persons), there is no ultimate contradiction between the true, the good, and the beautiful as found in psychology and as found in theology. Indeed, this synthesis of truth was envisioned by the fathers of the Second Vatican Council in their document *Gaudium et Spes*: "In pastoral care, sufficient use must be made, not only of theological principles, but also of the findings of the secular sciences, especially of psychology and sociology, so that the faithful may be brought to a more adequate and mature life of faith" (no. 62). Just as Thomas Aquinas incorporated the insights of Aristotle in order to come to a deeper understanding of Christian theology, so too the Christian psychologist of today can learn from the insights of psychology in gaining a greater understanding about the human person.

Psychology may even aid in the work of sharing faith. René Girard taught: "Man is the creature who does not know what to desire, and he turns to others in order to make up his mind. We desire what others desire because we imitate their desires."[7] In their book *Yes! 50 Scientifically Proven Ways to Be Persuasive*, Noah J. Goldstein, Steve J. Martin, and Robert B. Cialdini support Girard's view by pointing to empirical evidence in psychology of the "bandwagon effect."[8] What we think other people want is what we tend to want. So, it is helpful to emphasize models of good faith and practice (the saints) and the numbers of people who are doing the right thing. All people, but especially the young, want to fit in and do what they perceive to be "normal." In speaking to people of no faith or weak faith, it is counterproductive to evangelization to emphasize how many people reject Catholic faith and practice. It is much more helpful to emphasize the fact that "the Catholic Church is larger than any other single religious institution in the United States, with over 17,000 parishes that serve a large and diverse population."[9] In evangelizing less than fully committed audiences, it is useful to speak of modern conversion stories, the more than 2 million Catholics in the United States who attend Mass more than once a week, and the many young people who are attracted to practices such as Eucharistic Adoration.[10] It is, of course, necessary in some contexts (among highly committed Catholic leaders) to address the "bad news" of disaffiliation from the Catholic Church, but in the work of sharing faith the empirical psychological research indicates that it is much more helpful to find and emphasize the "good news" of conversions, faithfulness, and good work done by the Church.[11] Those seeking to evangelize need not fear psychology but may make judicious use of it. And yet, psychological considerations cannot replace the need for philosophy in sharing faith. This is particularly true when considering arguments for God's existence, to which we now turn.

Reasons for Belief in God

8

Does Beauty Point to God?

Plato's Way to the Divine

Plato wrote, "Beauty alone has this privilege, to be the most clearly visible and the most loved."[1] In the *Symposium*, Plato describes a ladder of love: First, an individual becomes attracted to a particular beautiful person. Next, the individual sees that beauty is possessed by other persons, by nature, and by society. Finally, an individual can arrive at "beauty absolute, separate, simple, and everlasting . . . without diminution and without increase, or any change."[2]

But what exactly is beauty? St. Thomas Aquinas taught that the beautiful is something pleasant to apprehend. He also taught that the greatest possible pleasure is enjoyed in heaven where the saints see God face-to-face. God is therefore the ultimate beauty because God gives the greatest pleasure when seen. Indeed, Thomas Aquinas argued that God is the true, the good, and the beautiful, the unity of the Forms sought by Plato.[3]

In her essay "Beauty as a Road to God," the contemporary philosopher Eleonore Stump notes that "very few people, maybe hardly any people, come to God because they are convinced by a proof. As far as I can see, people come to God because of something else entirely, not because of some convincing argument for God's existence but rather because of some desire or yearning in them."[4] This seems right. For every Alasdair MacIntyre or Edward Feser who comes to belief in God through philosophical argument, there are thousands of people whose faith in God is kindled by the beauty of holding a sleeping child.

Since the road to God is always a personal one, Stump points out, "Something will be a road to God for a person only in case it goes from the spiritual or psychological or moral place where that person is to the one objective destination which is God. And so although a road to God will have one fixed ending point, it will have as many different beginning points as there are people engaged in the process of coming to God."[5] Paul McCartney's "Let It Be" might be helpful for one person to move toward God (given her particular situation) but not another person. As Stump puts it, "A road to God has to start where the person traveling that road is. So only what you find beautiful can be the beauty which is a road to God for you."[6]

The road to God leads not to a physical place like Seattle but to a personal relationship like a marriage. Our relationships come in degrees of intimacy. We can be more or less close to God, as we can be more or less close to anyone else. Stump writes: "You cannot get a personal relationship with another person just by being in the same place as that person. You need also to have some meeting of minds and hearts, and there cannot be any such harmony of wills between a perfectly good God and a person whose will is not fixed in righteousness. It is in this way that there is distance between a human person and God."[7] Since God is unchangingly loving and good, the change must take place on the part of the human being.

So, how exactly does Stump think that beauty can help us in our journey to a closer relationship with God? First, beauty stokes desire. She writes:

> Sometimes beauty wakes in us a desire, a great yearning, an inchoate longing for something. . . . There is a strong connection between beauty and the desire which makes a heart restless until it surrenders to God. "Beauty" is a good name for what

> draws us when we feel such desire, when we feel restless in Augustine's sense. When we are in the grip of that Augustinian sort of desire, we often do not know what we are yearning for. But Augustine (as well as many others in the Christian tradition) thought that if both the beauty and the desire for it are real and great, then in effect the desire is a desire which will lead to God.[8]

Painful longing can help us move toward God, to allow God more deeply into our lives.

Second, the suffering that can take us away from God is eased by beauty, in particular by the beauty of sad music. Stump notes that this kind of music "gives us a sense of peace even in pain. It is, as it were, a redeemed pain. The whole effect is a stillness which is willing to trust God even in pain. This music thus mediates to us an acceptance of the pain in our innermost psyches. Those griefs, those failures, which might have bent us away from God in shame or anger lose some of their power to do so, in the quiet of the beauty of that music."[9] Beauty can melt us, ease our resistance to union with God, and console us in times of suffering.

And then there is the beauty that enhances our joy and gratitude to God. Stump writes: "It is important not to forget the way in which beauty in art can be just joyful. The choral part at the end of Beethoven's Ninth Symphony, for example, is a great overflowing of exuberance, of gratitude, hope, and joy. Here pain is simply absent, and there is a rush of gladness that lets us forget sorrow and trouble for a time. Gladness and joy in beauty also strengthen us for the road to God and draw us further on it."[10] So, beauty can be a road to God because "it arouses feelings in us which make us long for God's presence or produce in us peace even in a fallen world or render us joyful in the good we find around us."[11]

Stump concludes her essay with this comment: "Goodness presented to the senses is a kind of stealth bomber. It flies in under the radar of the reason to have its effect on desire, without a preemptive strike on the part of reason to stop it. By prompting pain in us, even pain of a redeemed or transcended sort, or by giving us the kind of love of goodness which is joy, beauty perceptible to the senses moves us to the goodness of God, who is himself beautiful, to see it."[12] Lewis made a similar observation: "The books or the music in which we thought the beauty was located will betray us if we trust [in] them; it was not in them, it only came through them, and what came through them was longing. These things—the beauty, the memory of our own past—are good images of what we really desire; but if they are mistaken for the thing itself they turn into dumb idols, breaking the hearts of their worshippers."[13] We need not an idol of beauty, but the God of Beauty.

Stump notes, "I do not say that beauty is *the* road to God. There are many roads to God, and different roads are appropriate for different people."[14] In this insight, she echoes the future Pope Benedict XVI, Joseph Ratzinger. He was once asked, "Are there many roads to God or just one?" The future pope answered, "There are as many ways as there are people."[15]

9

Are There Immaterial Realities?

Augustine's Way to God

Is it reasonable to believe that God exists? Although some people think that faith and reason are opposed to each other, another possibility is that faith and reason can work in harmony. We can have reasons for various faith claims, such as the claim that God exists. Aristotle, Anselm, Aquinas, Leibniz, and William Lane Craig provide famous reasons to believe that God exists, some of which we will explore in future chapters. Less well known is a way proposed by the African intellectual St. Augustine of Hippo. In his fascinating book *Five Proofs of the Existence of God*, Edward Feser explains this argument at length. Inspired by Augustine, let's begin with the reality that 2 + 2 = 4.

Some realities exist in matter. A house is made of wood, nails, and cement. A dog has fur, muscles, and bones. Other realities exist in a mind. My memories of seeing the Grateful Dead in concert and of running track against Harvard exist in my mind. Your beliefs about dogs and about chocolate exist in your mind.

Does the reality of 2 + 2 = 4 exist in matter or in mind? Well, material realities have a particular weight, length, and density. But the reality that 2 + 2 = 4 does not have a weight, a length, or a density. So, the reality that 2 + 2 = 4 does not exist as a material object.

Moreover, as we saw in chapter 4, 2 + 2 = 4 is not a material reality. Material realities depend on matter for their continued existence. When the snow melts, the snowman is gone. But 2 + 2 = 4 is not a reality that would cease to exist if someone burned all the math books. Mathematical truths can be represented in written symbols or spoken words. But the *reality* of mathematical truth does not depend on the *representation* of this truth. The reality of 2 + 2 = 4 was true before anyone wrote it down or said it. So, the reality that 2 + 2 = 4 does not exist as a material object but as a mental reality.

Mental realities depend on a mind for their existence. If my mind is destroyed, gone will be my memories of playing pick-up games at Northwest soccer camp with Michelle Akers and practicing jujitsu with Royce Gracie. If your mind is destroyed, your knowledge of your mom and your favorite food is destroyed along with it.

Yet, the reality that 2 + 2 = 4 is different because it would not be destroyed even if every human mind were destroyed. It was true *before* any human being knew about it. It would remain true even if all human beings ceased to exist. Mathematical realities like 2 + 2 = 4 are timeless, unchanging, intelligible, and true. So, since the reality of 2 + 2 = 4 is a timeless and unchanging reality, it does not depend upon a mind that is contingent, in time, and changeable. Rather, the reality of 2 + 2 = 4 must exist in a mind that does not come into existence and cannot fall out of existence, since 2 + 2 = 4 does not begin to be true, nor could 2 + 2 = 4 ever stop being true.

Moreover, 2 + 2 = 4 is not the only mathematical reality. Indeed, there are infinite mathematical realities simply in terms of addition (3 + 3 = 6, 4 + 4 = 8, 5 + 5 = 10, etc.). There are countless more mathematical realities of subtraction, multiplication, division, algebra, calculus, and so on. Indeed, there are innumerable truths that are timeless, unchanging, and intelligible. But only an infinite mind can know infinite realities, so it follows that there must exist a mind that is outside of time, not coming into existence, not having the possibility of going out of existence, which knows infinite realities. The word commonly used in English for a necessarily existing, eternally understanding, and infinitely knowing mind is *God*.

Now, at this point, someone might reply that 2 + 2 = 4 is *not* in fact an objective reality grounded in matter or in a mind. According to this view, 2 + 2 = 4 is merely a collection of symbols or ideas that human beings made up. Math is no more real than Cinderella's fairy godmother. Math is just a fictional story and does not give us factual truth.

But if math is not real, then science is not real. As Paul Davies points out, "The laws of physics . . . are all expressed as mathematical equations."[1] Take, for example, Newton's second law of motion: force equals mass times acceleration. Or consider Einstein's $E = mc^2$. These formulas depend upon the truth of multiplication. If mathematics does not give us objective truth, then science cannot give us objective truth.

In fact, the fictional story is that mathematics is *merely* words or ideas that human beings made up like a fairy tale. Cinderella's fairy godmother cannot physically move a Boeing 747 through the air from Los Angeles to Boston. Science can.

Science gives us objective truths that are independent of the human mind, making our technology possible. When humans realized that the sun is hotter than ice, they understood an objective truth. So, too, when the first human realized that 2 + 2 = 4, this person discovered an objectively true reality. Science is real. So math must be factual, not fictional.

In sum, it is an objective reality that 2 + 2 = 4. Mathematical realities don't exist as material objects with color, shape, and weight; rather, they exist in your mind and my mind. Mental realities depend on a mind for their existence. But the reality that 2 + 2 = 4 (like countless other mathematical facts) is a timeless reality and an unchanging truth, so it cannot depend upon minds like ours that come into existence and can go out of existence. So, there must exist a mind that is necessarily existing, eternally understanding, and infinitely knowing. This mind Augustine calls God.

10

What Caused the Universe?

An Islamic Way to God

First put forward by Islamic scholars in the Middle Ages, the Kalam cosmological argument for God's existence has two premises. The first is, "Whatever begins to exist has a cause." The second premise is, "The universe began to exist." If these two premises are true, the conclusion follows logically, "Therefore, the universe has a cause."

Let's take a look at the major premise: "Whatever begins to exist has a cause." There are a number of reasons to think that this premise is true, as the idea that whatever begins to exist has a cause is evident from our experience. We see a baby girl and know that she has a cause: her parents. We see a new puddle form in the backyard and know it has a cause: the recent rain.

The premise "whatever begins to exist has a cause" is used in our scientific explanations of the world. If there's a big forest fire, we don't say, "Oh, it just happened. Nothing caused that." We search for a cause. "Was it caused by a lightning strike? Was it caused by someone smoking? Was it caused by someone not tending a campfire properly?"

When we find a dead human body, we don't say, "Oh, death just happened. No cause of death to be investigated here." No, we ask, "What caused this death? Was the person murdered? Was it a heart attack? Was it cancer? What caused this person to go from being alive to being dead?"

All known scientific evidence confirms that whatever begins to exist has a cause. There's no evidence at all that some things begin to exist without a cause. So, we have all the inductive evidence in the world that the first premise of the Kalam argument is true.

And consider the alternative. Whatever begins to exist has no cause. Something comes into being from nothing. As William Lane Craig notes, "To claim that something can come into being from nothing is worse than magic. When a magician pulls a rabbit out of a hat, at least you've got the magician, not to mention the hat!"[1] So, it is reasonable to believe that whatever begins to exist has a cause.

The second premise of the Kalam cosmological argument is, "The universe began to exist." "Universe" here refers to all time, all space, and all matter. So, the second premise could be restated as, "All time, all space, and all matter began to exist." Is it true that the universe began to exist?

Aristotle, for example, thought that the universe was eternal, that it always existed. But we have learned a lot about the origin of the universe since the time of Aristotle. There's good reason to believe that the universe began to exist. Scientists, both atheist and theist, point to converging lines of evidence. Due to the radiation dispersal of the universe, scientists estimate that at one point in the past, about 13.7 billion years ago, all the known universe expanded outward. This expansion is sometimes called the Big Bang. Craig points out:

> There's actually a second scientific confirmation of the beginning of the universe, this one from the second law of thermodynamics. According to the second law, unless energy is being fed into a system, that system will become increasingly disorderly. . . .
>
> Already in the nineteenth century scientists realized that the second law implied a grim prediction for the future of the universe. Given enough time, all the energy in the universe

> will spread itself out evenly throughout the universe. . . . The universe will become a featureless soup in which no life is possible. Once the universe reaches such a state, no significant further change is possible. It is a state of equilibrium. . . . Scientists called this state of thermodynamic equilibrium the "heat death" of the universe.
>
> But this unwelcome prediction raised a further puzzle: If, given enough time, the universe *will* inevitably stagnate in a state of heat death, then why, if it has existed forever, is it not *now* in a state of heat death? If in a finite amount of time, the universe *will* reach equilibrium, then, given infinite past time, it should by now *already be* in a state of equilibrium. But it's not. We're in a state of disequilibrium, where energy is still available to be used and the universe has an orderly structure.[2]

If this universe had existed forever, then given the second law of thermodynamics, the universe would have run out of available energy. But it has not. The sun still shines; indeed, billions of stars still shine. So the universe has not, in fact, existed forever. Both radiation dispersal and the second law of thermodynamics point to a universe that began to exist.

Scientists have provided other evidence that points to the universe having a beginning. Evidence gathered from the Hubble Space Telescope also indicates that the universe began 13.7 billion years ago—another converging line of evidence from contemporary science.

Now, if it is true that time, space, and matter arose 13.7 billion years ago, then the universe did begin to exist. So, where does that leave us with respect to the Kalam cosmological argument? If the major premise is true, then all things with a beginning have a cause. If the minor premise is true, then the universe (all time, all space, and all matter) has a beginning. Therefore, the conclusion follows with logical necessity: the universe has a cause.

But let us now consider an objection to the Kalam argument. Maybe something can come into existence without a cause. Maybe all time, all space, and all matter caused itself to exist without

God. Could the universe cause itself to come into existence with no Creator? Imagine, if you will, someone who does not exist right now: your great-granddaughter. Let's call her Eunice. She does not now exist, and indeed she may never begin to exist. If Eunice does not exist, then she can do nothing. She can't get you coffee. She can't mow the lawn. And if she can't do *anything*, she can't cause anything. She can't cause the garbage to be taken out. She can't cause the window to open. She can't cause anything to change or to come into existence. If she can't cause anything at all, she can't cause herself to come into existence.

What is true of Eunice is also true of the universe. If the universe is 13.7 billion years old, then, prior to this point, there was no universe. There was no time. There was no space. There was no matter. But if the universe was nothing 14 billion years ago, then the universe could cause nothing. And if the universe can cause nothing, the universe can't cause itself to come into existence. So, just like your possible great-granddaughter, Eunice, the universe could not cause itself to come into existence. We need a cause for the universe that is beyond the universe. Similarly, your great-granddaughter Eunice needs to be caused by something beyond herself, if she is ever to come into existence. This raises a question.

Is the cause of the universe "God"?

Well, maybe yes, maybe no. It depends on what you mean by the term *God*. The cause of the universe has to be prior to time because the cause of the universe causes time to exist. So you might say the cause of the universe has to be something outside of time, something timeless, something eternal. The cause of the universe is also prior to matter and space, and so it has to be nonmaterial—or immaterial—and nonspatial.

Clearly, the cause of the universe also has to be something immensely powerful. Think about how much power it takes to make an aircraft carrier. It takes numerous welders, designers, and a huge manufacturing plant to make an enormous aircraft carrier. But to make the whole universe—to make all time, all space, all matter, all planets, all suns, everything—well, that takes immense power, unbelievable power.

Finally, we can ask, is the cause of the universe an impersonal cause or a personal cause? Consider an impersonal cause, like the sun. The sun nonvoluntarily causes whatever it causes, like emitting rays of heat and light. The sun doesn't wake up in the morning and decide, "Well, today, I'm going to give off light or be hot." No. The sun is an impersonal cause. It automatically does what it does, acts as it acts, heating and giving off light. Likewise, ice is an impersonal cause. As long as ice exists, it is cold and hard. If ice comes in contact with us, it causes us to become cooler.

By contrast, you and I are examples of personal causes. We choose to do some things and not other things. Sometimes we get up, and sometimes we sit down. Sometimes we speak; other times we are silent. We decide to leave for a trip on July 13, but not on June 20. Is the cause of the universe an impersonal cause like the sun or a personal cause like us?

Well, the cause of the universe was not always causing the universe. The cause of the universe began causing the universe almost 14 billion years ago but was not causing the universe 20 billion years ago. Unlike an impersonal cause like the sun, which always casts rays of light, the Cause of the universe was not always causing the universe.

So, is the cause of the universe God?

What would you call a cause that is timeless and eternal, a cause that is immaterial, a cause that is immensely powerful, and a cause that voluntarily brings about all time, all space, and all matter? Well, the word in English that we use to describe the timeless, immaterial, eternal, immensely powerful, and personal cause of the universe is *God*. Other languages use different terms for the same Entity. In Arabic, it's "Allah." In German, it's "Gott." In French, it's "Dieu." In Latin, it's "Deus."

Of course, you don't have to use any of these names; you could call this being the Creator, you could call this being the One who brought about the universe. But many people in English call the being that corresponds to an eternal, immaterial, immensely powerful, personal cause of the universe God. I'll continue to speak of God, but feel free to substitute in your mind "Creator" or "First Cause" or "an immensely powerful, immaterial, nonspatial cause of all time, all space, and all matter" if those terms suit you better.

Does the Kalam argument prove that the Christian God exists?

The Kalam cosmological argument does not take sides in a kind of interreligious dispute. In other words, Christians, Muslims, Jews, and Deists all would accept that the cause of the universe is God, even though they would all disagree about what God has done in history. Did God reveal himself fully in Christ? That is a question about which Christians, Muslims, Jews, and Deists do not agree. Yet they can all accept the Kalam cosmological argument, which is neutral with respect to the interreligious question about the identity of Jesus.

Now, someone might object, "Well, what caused God? If everything has a cause, what caused God?" But recall that the premise of the Kalam argument is *not* that "Everything has a cause" or "Everything has a beginning." The premise is, "Everything that *begins* has a cause." If I claim, "Every student *in this classroom* has a book," I am not claiming "Every student has a book." Likewise, to claim "everything has a cause" is very different from claiming "everything *with a beginning* has a cause."

The question "What caused God?" is a question that does not actually make sense. There are lots of questions that do not make sense, if you understand the terms that make up those questions. Let's say I ask, "How long is the color yellow? Is it three feet long? Is it four feet long?" How would you respond? In fact, the color yellow does not have any length. Likewise, if God is the cause of time, and therefore timeless, it doesn't make any sense to say, "*When* was God made?"

Either atheism is true, and there is no God, or atheism is not true, and there is a God. But either way, the question "What caused God?" makes no sense.

If atheism is right, there is no answer to the question "Who caused God?" Why? Well, because if atheism is right, there is no God. But the question "Who caused God?" wouldn't make sense if there were no such being as God. It would be like the question "Who is the grandmother of Santa Claus?" The supposition of "Who caused God?" is that God is something that came into existence, something that got caused. But if atheism is right, God is not something that came into existence.

On the other hand, theists believe God is an uncaused cause. So certainly in the theistic view, the question "Who caused God?" also doesn't make sense. God is an *un*caused cause. So, the question "Who caused God?" presupposes a supposition that is false: that God got caused.

So, whether atheism is true or theism is true, the question "Who made God?" is a nonsense question. It's a question like "How much does the number four weigh?" or "How can triangles make a snowman?" Such questions misunderstand the concepts involved.

Here's another objection to the Kalam cosmological argument. "Look, part of your argument is based on contemporary science, and science always advances and changes. What if the scientific evidence you appeal to is shown by later discoveries to be wrong?"

I don't know what science is going to reveal in the future. Maybe *The New York Times* is going to run a headline next month: "Universe Is Actually Eternal, Big Bang Never Happened." Maybe the radiation readings are all off. Maybe the second law of thermodynamics does not apply. Maybe the multiple converging lines of evidence pointing to a beginning are all wrong. Who knows what science will discover in the future? What if contemporary science is wrong?

This objection relies on faith that science in the future will undermine the conclusions of science today. It is a faith-based argument, not one based on evidence. A theist can just as well say, "Well, what if the science of the future provides much stronger grounds for holding that the universe has a beginning?" After all, the past fifty years of scientific research has provided more and more evidence for the beginning of the universe. So, why not assume that science will continue on this path with new discoveries only confirming and making even more precise the exact age of the universe?

But for the sake of argument, let's assume that scientists do find evidence that the universe had no beginning. Could we still use reason to argue for God's existence? In the next chapter, we will look at arguments that Thomas Aquinas gives for the existence of a First Cause and Unmoved Mover. Thomas thinks we don't have to rely on the premise "the universe began to exist." He argues that even if it were true that the universe was eternal, there would still have to be a First Cause and Unmoved Mover.

11

What is Causing the Universe to Continue to Exist?

St. Thomas Aquinas's Argument for an Unmoved Mover and an Uncaused Cause

In our previous chapter, we looked at the Kalam cosmological argument. The first premise of the argument is, "Whatever begins to exist has a cause." The minor premise of this argument is, "The universe began to exist." If these two premises are true, then the conclusion follows logically: "The universe has a cause."

In the thirteenth century, Dominican thinker Thomas Aquinas disagreed with the Kalam cosmological argument. He thought that you couldn't use philosophy to prove that the universe had a beginning. He believed as a matter of faith that the universe was not eternal. But he thought as a matter of philosophy, as a matter of the science of his time, that you could not show that the universe had a beginning.

But Thomas maintained that there are actually good reasons to think that God exists, with no appeal to the beginning of the universe needed. Faith and reason are in harmony, both pointing to God's existence. Although Thomas discusses arguments for God's existence in a number of his works, he put forward his famous "five ways" to argue for God's existence in his *Summa Theologiae*. This text is one of the most influential in the history of philosophy.

In this chapter, we will look at two of Thomas's five ways: the way from motion and the way from causality.

The Way from Motion

Aquinas's first way to argue for the existence of God is from motion.[1] The argument goes like this: It is evident that there is motion in the world. Thomas notes that whatever is moved is moved by another. Then he argues that there cannot be an infinite regress in movers, and therefore there must be a first mover, which is called God. Let's break this down.

What is motion? Thomas defines *motion* as the act of a being in potency insofar as it is in potency. What does that mean? Imagine a woman jogging on a trail. When she was at the beginning of the trail, she had the potential to be halfway down the trail, a potential that was not yet actualized. As she runs down the trail, she realizes or actualizes that potential. Once she's at the middle of the trail, she has actualized being in the middle of the run, but she still has the potential to be even farther down the trail. When she reaches the end of the trail, she will have actualized the entire run and will no longer be in motion. Motion is, you might say, a middle point between potency and act. When something moves, it goes from potentially being somewhere to actually being somewhere.

Motion, as Thomas uses the term, need not be a change in location. Let's say I have a pot of water. The water is actually at room temperature, but then I put the pot on a hot stove. The potency of the water to boil becomes actualized. So, the water changes. At first, it is actually at room temperature and only potentially boiling, but when the fire is applied underneath it, it changes and becomes actually boiling water. *Motion* is Thomas's word for that change, the actualization of potency.

Thomas then points out that whatever is moved is moved by another. Water at room temperature does *not* change into boiling water unless some heating cause—such as a hot stove—acts on the water. A house doesn't go from potentially being painted to actually being painted unless painters apply the paint.

Aquinas says that there can't be an infinite regress in movers. This idea might be illustrated by a train with ten cars heading up a hill. The last car in the train, the caboose, is pulled along by the ninth car in the train, the ninth car is pulled along by the eighth, the eighth by the seventh, and so on. The first car of the train, the locomotive, is pulling uphill all ten cars in the chain of the train. If that locomotive were to totally stop heading uphill, the motion of all the cars in the train would also stop. The whole chain of train cars is being pulled along by that first mover, that initial locomotive. If there were no locomotive pulling the train along, the rest of the train would not move. An intermediate mover can only move because it is itself moved by another. Its power is derivative. But if there is no first mover, then there is no second mover, or third, and so forth through the chain of *per se* movers. If there were no mover moving and causing change, there would be no change in the universe. But there is motion and change in the universe, so there must be a first mover, which people call God.

An objector *might* now say, "So, if everything moves, what moves God?" Aquinas does *not* say that everything is in motion. He says only that *some* things are in motion. Nor does he say that everything is moved by something else, but only that whatever is in motion is moved by something else. He's not claiming that *everything* is in motion or that *everything* is being moved. Aquinas's premises do not say and do not imply that God has to be changing like everything else or that he must be moved like everyone else. In this way, the Unmoved Mover is unlike the locomotive, which is itself moving.

The Way from Causality

Let's now look at Thomas's argument for God as the Uncaused Cause.[2] Let me state the argument briefly and then unpack it: First, there are some things that are caused. Everything caused is caused by another. Either there's an infinite regress in causes or there is an uncaused cause. Aquinas argues that there cannot be an infinite regress of causes. Therefore, there has to be an uncaused cause. Let's break all this down.

The first premise is that some things are caused. A baby is caused to come into existence by her mother and father. A bottle of water is caused by the company that makes it. Everything you see around you now is an example of something caused.

The second premise is that everything caused is caused by another. So, the baby is something that was caused, and the baby was caused by another, namely by mom and dad. So, everything that's caused to come into existence has to be caused by something else. Aquinas is here speaking of an efficient cause, which he understands as that which brings something into being or in some way alters a being that already exists.

Nothing can cause itself to come into existence, as I noted in the previous chapter. So if something is going to come into existence, it has to be caused by something else.

Now there is a very important distinction that is not explicitly made in Aquinas's argument as found in the Summa *Theologiae* that is vital to understanding his argument. Thomas assumed his readers would already know it, and we have already mentioned it in this chapter. This distinction is between two kinds of efficient causes, *per accidens* causes and *per se* causes. What's the difference? In a *per accidens* cause, the initial cause can go away, and the effects of that cause continue. So, if a man and a woman make a baby, the baby can continue to live even if both parents die. A sculptor is a *per accidens* cause of a sculpture. He can stop sculpting, but the effect of the sculpture remains.

By contrast, with *per se* causality, if any link in the chain is eliminated, all the subsequent links in the chain also cease to exist. But when a ballerina stops dancing, her dance ends. She is the *per se* cause of her dancing. All the effects in a *per se* order of causality depend on the cause *continuing to cause* the effect. If the song is going to continue, a singer needs to continue singing. When there is no singer singing, the song ceases to be sung.

Here's another example of *per se* causality. Let's say there is a bottle filled with water on a table. The water is being caused to exist where it is by the bottle. Now if you get rid of the bottle, if you melt it or blow it up or whatever, the water is not going to float in midair; it's going to fall to the ground. And the bottle itself is being caused right now to exist where it is. It's being caused by the table. So if you get rid of the table, well, that will get rid of the bottle being where it is, and that will get rid of the water being where it is. So, the water is being caused to be in its location by the bottle, the bottle is being caused to be where it is by the table, and eliminating either one of those is going to disrupt the location of the water. That's a *per se* order of causality. If you eliminate the earlier links in the chain, you eliminate the subsequent links.

Aquinas recognizes that *per se* causality is asymmetric. Whatever causal power a subsequent cause has derives from the prior cause. The first link is instrumental to the subsequent links.

Take the example of a plant in a hanging basket coming down from a chain attached to the ceiling. The link of the chain closest to the hanging plant can only hold up the plant if the first link holds strong. If the first link were not there, the second link couldn't hold the plant. And if the second link were not there, then the third link would have no causal power to hold up the next link, and so on. The plant existing where it is depends on there being a first link in the chain, since each subsequent link depends upon the prior links, however many there are.

Causality applies also to you and me. What causes you to exist right now? In the *per accidens* causal order, what caused you to come into existence were your parents, and your parents were caused by your grandparents, and so on.

What causes you to continue to exist in the *per se* order? Even if your parents die, you can still continue existing. But there are some things that are causing you to exist *right now* in the *per se* order of causality. So what are those things?

We need oxygen in order to continue to exist right now. We can't survive long without oxygen. Likewise, we need atmospheric pressure. If atmospheric pressure were to radically change, that would instantly kill us. If we were to take you to the bottom of the ocean right now, you would die right away. The pressure at the bottom of the ocean is so strong it would instantly crush you.

We're being caused to exist right now. We are caused not just by our parents in the *per accidens* order, but also caused right here and now. So what's causing us to exist? Among many things, atmospheric pressure. Now, what causes atmospheric pressure to exist? In other words, why is the atmospheric pressure what it is? Why is atmospheric pressure on the surface of the earth not like what it is at the bottom of the sea or like what it is in outer space?

Well, one of the things causing atmospheric pressure is the temperature. In other words, atmospheric pressure changes if the temperature changes. If the temperature got much hotter, like that of the surface of the sun, the atmospheric pressure would change. We would die. Imagine if the temperature were a lot colder, absolute zero, −459.67°F. Again, we could not live. One of the causes that is needed for us to continue to live is that the temperature stay within a certain range, not too hot and not too cold. So, one *per se* cause of us, the atmospheric pressure, is itself being caused. Temperature is something that changes, and temperature is itself being caused.

To sum up, you and I are caused by atmospheric pressure, among other things. In turn, atmospheric pressure is itself being caused by temperature, among other things. Temperature is also being caused. So, what we have is an essentially ordered series, a *per se* ordering.

An intermediate and derivative cause (like atmospheric pressure or the temperature) derives its causal power from one or more prior causes. Now if there were only intermediate and derivative causes, then there would be no source from which all the causal powers of the intermediate causes could be derived. If there were only intermediate causes, then the intermediate causes would be powerless to cause the things that they're causing. The derivative cause would not be able to cause anything. But we clearly know that the derivative and intermediate causes can cause things. The temperature is causing atmospheric pressure. The atmospheric pressure is causing us to continue to exist.

So, there cannot be *only* derivative causes, intermediate causes. There has to be something that is an underived cause, a first cause, an uncaused cause.

You might liken it to sharing a pizza. Let's say we are sitting around a table and someone brings a large pizza for us to share. You take a piece and hand the pizza on to the next person, they take a piece and hand it on to the next person, they take a piece and hand it on to the next person, and so on. Unless someone brings the pizza to start with, there is no pizza to be shared. Unless someone brings the causal power to start with, there can't be the causal power to be shared. There can't be, in other words, only derivative causes.

That is why there can't be an infinite regress in *per se* causes. A cause is either in itself uncaused, or itself also caused. And if a cause is itself being caused, like atmospheric pressure, then we've not yet explained what caused the thing that we're trying to explain. So, if we were trying to figure out, for instance, why human beings continue to exist, and then we appeal to atmospheric pressure, which is itself being caused, we're simply restating the problem of explanation at a different level. So a sufficient explanation demands that there be an uncaused cause.

An objection to Aquinas's argument was once posed by one of the most famous intellectuals of the twentieth century, the atheist philosopher Bertrand Russell. He objected to the second way of arguing for God's existence, saying, "If everything has a cause, what caused God?"[3] What would Aquinas say to this objection? How would he respond to this objection? I don't know for sure.

But if you read Thomas's argument carefully, you see that Thomas does *not* say everything has a cause. Rather, he says everything *that is caused* is caused by another. He simply does not hold that everything is caused. Indeed, Thomas explicitly denies that every being is caused by another in the *Summa Contra Gentiles* (II.52.5). Thomas says something different. He says everything that is being caused is caused by another. That's a totally different claim than to say everything is caused. To claim "all people *in this room* speak English" is totally different from claiming that "all people speak English."

We can now summarize Thomas's argument. First, there are some things that are being caused. You, me, dogs, trees, and so on. Second, everything that's being caused in the *per se* order is being caused by something else. Nothing can cause itself. Either there's an infinite regress in causes or there is an uncaused cause. There can't be an infinite regress in causes since intermediate and derivative causes provide no sufficient explanation of their own causal power. Therefore, there has to be an uncaused cause, which people call God.

12

Are Faith and Reason Opposed?

A Critique of Richard Dawkins

According to Richard Dawkins, faith and reason are totally opposed to each other. Religious believers are delusional for believing in God because it is a belief without any rational justification. Dawkins dedicates a large section of his book *The God Delusion* to a philosophical critique of Thomas Aquinas's and others' arguments for God's existence.

The preface to the paperback edition of *The God Delusion* contains a response to critics in which Dawkins offers rebuttals to the robust, sometimes scathing, criticism of the first edition. Each criticism is summarized in a sentence, such as, "You can't criticize religion without a detailed analysis of learned books of theology," followed by a few paragraphs from Dawkins in response. His response to this particular criticism is instructive: "I would happily have forgone bestseller-dom if there had been the slightest hope of Duns Scotus illuminating my central question of whether God exists. The vast majority of theological writings simply assume that he does, and go on from there. For my purposes, I need consider only those theologians who take seriously the possibility that God does not exist and argue that he does."[1]

In fact, Scotus is one such theologian. He provides a number of philosophical arguments in at least four different works—all of which are simply ignored by Dawkins. Scotus's arguments are not based on faith or revelation or personal "religious experience" but rather on what can be known through reason. Dawkins "knows" prior to investigation that Scotus can teach him nothing about the question of God's existence without even being aware that Scotus addresses the question.[2] This assumption amounts to a close-minded dogmatism.

Also missing in *The God Delusion* is any consideration of contemporary philosophers such as Alvin Plantinga, John Haldane, Robert Adams, and William Lane Craig, who all offer philosophical (not theological) arguments for God's existence. I rather doubt Dawkins would take kindly to a critique of biology that ignored the work of virtually all prominent contemporary biologists and only selectively treated their predecessors. To ignore such philosophers and their arguments—with the claim that one need not be an expert in leprechaunology to dismiss belief in leprechauns—is to beg the question.

The God Delusion also ignores or is unaware of medieval and contemporary forms of the *Kalam* argument for God's existence, which we looked at in chapter 10. The *Kalam* argument poses significant difficulties for Dawkins and other atheists who accept that science can reveal the truth about the world. The first premise—whatever begins to exist has a cause—seems to be presupposed by scientific inquiry itself, which, in part, investigates how things come to be. The second premise—the universe began to exist—is itself accepted as scientifically justified by the evidence of the expansion and cooling of the universe. Given the premises, the truth of the conclusion logically follows. The universe has a cause, and the name most cultures give to the cause of the universe is God. So, how does Dawkins critique this argument? He simply ignores it or is unaware of it.

Inductive Fallacy

Dawkins does offer a rebuttal to each of St. Thomas's five ways of demonstrating God's existence. His exposition, however, reveals that he does not understand the thought of the Angelic Doctor. To show that a proposition is mistaken requires that the position first be understood. We cannot refute what we do not understand.

Although Dawkins correctly notes that the first three ways—from movement, causality, and contingency—share a rejection of infinite regress, he misunderstands both the particulars and the larger metaphysical context of Thomas's five ways.

Take, for example, Dawkins's summary of Thomas's proof from causality: "Nothing is caused by itself. Every effect has a prior cause, and again we are pushed back into regress. This has to be terminated by a first cause, which we call God." A careful reader will note that Dawkins's formulation of Thomas differs from Thomas's actual argument. Thomas denies that there can be an infinite regress in *per se efficient causes*, but he does not deny that there can be infinite regress in other respects or that some kinds of regress terminate in a natural being.

Dawkins provides no argument in favor of infinite regress of any kind; he does not deny this premise to Thomas. Quite to the contrary, he points out that:

> some regresses do reach a natural terminator. Scientists used to wonder what would happen if you could dissect, say, gold into the smallest possible pieces. Why shouldn't you cut one of those pieces in half and produce an even smaller smidgen of gold? The regress in this case is decisively terminated by the atom. The smallest possible piece of gold is a nucleus consisting of exactly 79 protons and a slightly larger number of neutrons, attended by a swarm of electrons. If you "cut" gold any further than the level of the single atom, whatever you get is not gold.[3]

Just as gold ends in a natural terminator of a single atom, so too regress toward the first cause can end in a natural terminator.

The unstated premise of Dawkins's argument is that since some regresses (splitting the gold) end in a natural terminator, all regresses must end in a natural terminator. This is an example of the inductive fallacy. Just because *some* men are born in Spain, it does not follow that *all* men are born in Spain. Likewise, even if some regresses end in a natural terminator, it need not follow that *all* regresses end in a natural terminator. Dawkins has given us an example of a regress ending in a natural terminator; he has given us no reason to think that all regresses end in a natural terminator.

The Cause of It All

Further, Dawkins's example is irrelevant to Thomas's argument from causality, movement, or being. Consider the argument from causality. If we have a piece of gold and split it in half, it is not the case that one half of the piece causes the other half of the piece to exist. One half of the piece could be destroyed and the other half would continue to exist. There is simply no causal link between the two pieces of gold. By contrast, Thomas is talking about chains of causality in which the removal of one link in the chain would cause the other links in the chain to cease to exist. To repeat our example from chapter 11, you and I are (right now) caused to exist by atmospheric pressure. If atmospheric pressure were to cease to exist or change radically, we too would cease to exist—as would happen if we were on the moon without a space suit or at the bottom of the ocean without a submarine. Likewise, atmospheric pressure is itself something that is caused to exist by further caused beings: temperature, air density, altitude, and relative humidity. If these factors were to change radically or be removed, then atmospheric pressure would change radically or cease to exist. These factors themselves are caused to exist by still other factors, and so on.

Thomas's point about this causal chain of existence is that it must terminate in something that has existence not from another but rather from itself. The causal chain that causes us to exist is entirely unlike one lump of gold that is split into two small lumps. Without air density, atmospheric pressure ceases to exist. Without atmospheric pressure, we cease to exist. Without the one small lump of gold, the other small lump of gold can continue to exist.

Dawkins's example is irrelevant and misses Thomas's point about causal relationships.

Dawkins also objects that even if we admit a terminator of the regress in causation or explanation, "there is absolutely no reason to endow that terminator with any of the properties normally ascribed to God: omnipotence, omniscience, goodness, creativity in design, to say nothing of such human attributes as listening to prayers, forgiving sins, and reading innermost thoughts."[4] In other words, even if there is a first cause, this cause need not be God as understood in the traditional sense with all the attributes ascribed to the Divinity.

On this score, Thomas would agree with Dawkins insofar as the five ways were never intended to be a full description of all that can be claimed about God through rational argumentation. True, most people would call the origin of the universe, the first cause, "God," but Thomas would agree that the five ways do not, of themselves, show that God enjoys perfection, omnipotence, omniscience, goodness, and creativity. Dawkins's critique amounts to the fact that in a single article (the smallest complete subsection of the *Summa*), Thomas's work does not show all that can be shown rationally about God. This is rather like critiquing a biology textbook because it does not lay out all that can be known about biology in the first two pages.

For this reason, in both the *Summa Theologiae* and the *Summa Contra Gentiles* (whose complex argument for God's existence Dawkins completely ignores), Thomas goes on to argue that the first cause must be a Being without composition, without beginning or end, without change, and without evil (intellectual or moral) of any kind. These divine attributes are corollaries that can be deduced from the notion of an uncaused cause. We will address these divine attributes (e.g., omniscience, omnibenevolence) in future chapters of this book.

Dawkins is an excellent scientist. But he fails badly as a philosopher. It is not just that he misunderstands and provides fallacious critiques of Thomas's five ways. It is not just that there is no evidence in *The God Delusion* that he understands or is even aware of prominent contemporary philosophers of religion who argue in favor of God's existence. His fundamental problem is that he is ignorant of his own ignorance. He appears closed to wonder about the deepest questions in life, questions that the empirical method of science cannot answer. Dawkins oversteps his scientific knowledge in the delusion that such training makes him competent to judge dogmatically the deepest philosophical and religious questions.

So, if Aquinas is right, there must exist an Unmoved Mover and an Uncaused Cause. So far, we have *not* said anything about whether this God is perfect, all-good, eternal, or anything else. But what can we know about this God? Can we know anything more about God? Those are very good questions that we will explore in upcoming chapters. But first we will consider what God is not.

13

Can We Know What God Is Not?

The Way of Remotion

In this chapter, I will address what we can know about God primarily by means of challenging mistaken understandings of God. First, I'll look at what Thomas calls *the way of remotion*. Next, using the way of remotion, I'll consider God as eternal. Finally, I'll examine the idea that God is not composed. As we will see, faith and reason are in harmony, not disagreement, about these matters.

The Way of Remotion

Previously, I looked at how Aquinas moves from effects in the world to God as the First Cause of the world. We proceed from effects to cause in many investigations. For example, art historians examine Michelangelo's painting *The Last Judgment* to understand better the artist Michelangelo.

So, what can we know about God? How does Aquinas think that we can come to know things about God? Well, one of the prime ways is through what he calls the way of remotion. This is also called *apophatic theology* or *negative theology*.

So, what is the way of remotion? We can avoid misunderstandings about what God *is* by understanding what God *is not*. Imagine a detective. A detective begins to solve a crime by compiling a list of possible suspects. Let's say there are five or six people who he thinks could have done the murder. The detective will interview each one and check out their location during the time of the crime. Hopefully, the detective will be able to eliminate various suspects. He'll say, "Well, Mary couldn't have done the murder, because she was off at cross-country camp. And George couldn't have done the murder, because he was busy waiting tables. And John Paul couldn't do the murder, because he was serving in the Marines overseas." As the detective goes through the list of suspects, eliminating those who could not have done the murder, the detective gets closer to solving the crime.

Aquinas thinks that we can come to a more accurate understanding of who God is by trying to understand what God is *not*. By eliminating misunderstandings about who God is, we become less ignorant of God. This elimination of misunderstandings about the Divine is called the way of remotion.

God Has No Limit

So, here's one way God is *not* like us. Each of us has a limit to our life. We did not live two hundred years ago. And, unless there are radical advances in medicine, we will not still be alive two hundred years from now. Our coming into existence and going out of existence indicate that our existence has limits.

Aquinas holds that God's existence is not limited, that he is eternal. To say God is eternal is to say that God is lacking a terminus. God has limitless existence—no beginning, no coming into existence. And God also has no end, no leaving existence.

Why does Aquinas think that God is eternal? Well, if God is really the *Uncaused* Cause as we talked about in chapter 11, then God can't have a beginning. Everything with a beginning requires a cause. Nothing can cause itself to come into existence. Whatever begins to exist has a cause. So, since the Uncaused Cause is not caused, the Uncaused Cause does not begin to exist. He has no limit of a beginning.

And if God is the Unmoved Mover, then God can never cease existing. When we move from being alive to being dead, we're changed in some way. The cause of a person's death makes the person go from being alive to no longer being alive.

But if God has no potentiality to be actualized, if God is pure actuality, then God cannot be moved or changed from existing to not existing. And if God is really *un*caused, then nothing can *cause* God to stop existing. So, God has no beginning. God has no ceasing to be. In other words, God is eternal.

Likewise, if the Kalam cosmological argument is sound, then God must be timeless. God is the cause of time, so he must be prior to time. But anything that exists unbounded and unlimited by time is eternal. So, God is eternal.

Aquinas points out that God's eternal nature is confirmed by scripture. The psalmist says, "Before the mountains were born or you brought forth the whole world, from everlasting to everlasting you are God" (Ps 90:2, NIV). God was in the beginning, is now, and ever shall be. This is one of many examples of the harmony of faith and reason. Faith teaches that God is eternal, not having a beginning and not having an end. And philosophical reason can also establish that God is eternal, having no beginning and never ceasing to be.

Understanding God as eternal is important, for God's eternity allows him to relate to us in a way beyond what any human being can do. Human beings in time can only relate to us in a time-limited way. They must divide their time between us and others. But God, being eternal and outside of time, is not so limited. As Eleonore Stump points out:

> God is outside of time, and we are limited to time. Somewhat counterintuitively, God is actually *more* present to us than we are to each other. This is because God is present to every instant of our lives at once, and all the time. We interact with each other in a limited way, only in the temporal present. God's eternal simultaneity with our temporal present means that God is present with us each moment from the temporal past, present, and future, all at once as an eternal present.[1]

Since God is always present to us, we can have a deeper and richer relationship with God than with a limited human being. God is not limited by time. So, God is more free to relate to us than any time-bound person.

God Is Not Composed

So too, Aquinas also argues that God is not composed. What does that mean? Well, there's no potentiality in God. Potency means an aptitude to change, to be acted upon, to receive some new determination. A house has a potency to be painted a different color. You have the potency to gain weight or to lose weight. (I seem to have a stronger potency to gain than to lose, but that's another matter.)

My physical composition is something that leads me to be a contingent being. Since I'm composed of parts, I can be decomposed, as happens after death. Similarly, a car is composed of various parts, and therefore a car is also a contingent being. The car can go out of existence if we take the car apart.

So, composed beings are contingent beings. What is composed can in principle be decomposed. So, if God were composed, he could also be decomposed and go out of existence. But, as we just established, God is eternal and cannot go out of existence. So, God cannot be composed. Another way of saying that God is not composed is to say that God is simple. The divine simplicity and the lack of composition of God are two ways of stating the same reality.

Furthermore, Aquinas argues that what is composed needs a composer. What does that mean? Well, think about a car. A car needs to be put together by a car company. There needs to be a human being or a machine bringing the wheels, the brakes, and the windows all together. A car is a car, rather than just an unassembled heap of car parts, only if it is composed.

Composed beings need some prior cause that brings them into existence and composes them. But if God is really the first *uncaused* cause, there can't be anything prior to God that composes God. And so, God is not a composed being.

If God is not composed, then God cannot be like us, composed partly of potency and partly of actuality. I'm actually about 180 pounds, but I could potentially become 200 pounds or 160 pounds. If God is not composed of potentiality and actuality, then either God is only potentiality or God is only actuality.

But God could not be *only* potentiality. My great-granddaughter does not exist right now. But she might exist someday. For now, she is merely potential. What is *merely* potential, nonexisting, like my great-granddaughter, cannot do anything or cause anything. But if God is a cause, the Uncaused Cause, then God must be actual. And if God is not composed of act and potency, then God must be pure actuality.

God has no potency to change. So, is God like a stone statue that sits there unchanging? Not in the least. In a later chapter, we will examine the idea that God never ceases his loving activity, his willing of the good, his knowing of the truth. God is pure activity, maximal action, utmost energy. God is, therefore, almost maximally *unlike* a fixed statue. The statue doesn't move anything, doesn't know anything, and doesn't love anything. The statue passively receives the rain and birds that land on it. By contrast, God actively causes in his eternal activity as the ultimate First Cause the rain, birds, and the statue itself. God knows and loves all creation. God is pure actuality, not composed of actuality and potency. God is not unchanging like a statue.

Knowing that God is not a composed being helps us to avoid misunderstanding God. I remember attending a conference at a university, and the theme of the conference was "What Color Is God?" What would Aquinas say about this question?

I think he'd say that this question makes no sense. It's a little bit like the question "How long is the color yellow?" Well, the color yellow is no particular length. The question "How long is the color yellow?" doesn't make sense if you understand what the color yellow is.

Likewise, the question "What color is God?" makes no sense if you understand what God is not. God is not composed, so God does not have a body made up of various parts. Consider your own body. You've got arms and legs and a heart and a liver. Bodies by their nature are composed of parts. So, you are a composite being. But as we've shown, God is not composite. And therefore, God is also not a body. And because God doesn't have a body, God can't have a body that is any particular color.

God is not, in Aquinas's view, an old white man with a beard in the sky. God is not an old black man like Morgan Freeman in *Bruce Almighty.* God is not a woman; God is not a child. God is not a body at all, and therefore God doesn't have a color at all.

So, Aquinas notes, reason again agrees with scripture. Reason shows that God is not a bodily, composed being. Likewise, the Bible teaches that "God is spirit" (Jn 4:24). Faith and reason are in harmony, not disagreement.

God Does Not Have Accidents

Here's another instance of the way of remotion. Thomas holds that God does not have any accidental characteristics. What does this mean? Thomas is using Aristotle's distinction between substance and accidents. We can illustrate this by means of a particular human being, Socrates. Socrates is, you might say, substantially—or in his substance—a human being. He's not a dog or a cat or a tree.

Socrates also has what Aristotle calls "accidents." Accidental characteristics, for Aristotle, have nothing to do with chance events like a car accident. These are nonsubstantial characteristics such as being bald or snub-nosed or weighing 175 pounds. So, you can distinguish between what Socrates is in himself—he's a human—and the accidental characteristics of Socrates that come and go. When Socrates was ten years old, he wasn't bald. When he was a newborn baby, he didn't weigh 175 pounds. These accidental characteristics can change, but Socrates remains Socrates. He remains the same human being substantially.

We all have characteristics that in Aristotle's terms would be called accidental. For instance, we might be tan right now, but we may become pale during the winter months. We might be in good shape right now, but we may lose our fitness if we become sedentary. All these things would be accidental characteristics.

But for us, substantially, we're human beings from the very beginning of our life to the very end of our life. We never change from being human into being a dog or a cat or a tree. We're human for as long as we live. By contrast, our accidental characteristics, like our skin being tan, are things that can come and go.

So, for Aquinas, a substance is that which exists in itself, not in some subject or as part of anything else. By contrast, accidents cannot exist on their own but only as part of some substance.

Are there accidental characteristics in God? Well, either something causes the accidents in God, as, say, the sun causes me to get tan, or one part of God acts on another part of God to cause those accidents. But both of those are impossible.

There can't be something else causing something in God, because God is the First Cause, the Uncaused Cause. And one part of God can't act on another part of God, because God is not composed of parts; God doesn't have one part that could act on another part. So, by way of remotion, Thomas recognizes that in God, there are no accidental characteristics.

Accidents, moreover, presuppose potencies. That is to say, my accidental characteristic to become tan presupposes that I have the potency of gaining a tan. So, if you have no potency, you'll have no accidental characteristics that ride piggyback, as it were, on top of the potency. God has no potency. So, there are no accidental characteristics in God.

If Aquinas is right, then God is quite unlike anything in our experience. God is *Totaliter Aliter*, Totally Other. Everything we see is a combination of act and potency. Everything we sense is composed of parts. God is beyond all that.

14

Are We All Atheists?

The "One God Further" Objection

Richard Dawkins said, "We are all atheists about most of the gods that humanity has ever believed in. Some of us just go *one god further.*"[1] As the philosopher Bill Vallicella put it, "Given that everyone is an atheist with respect to some gods, one may as well make a clean sweep and be an atheist with respect to all gods."[2]

The "one God further" objection is aimed at minimizing the differences between atheism and theism. The difference between theism and atheism is just one. Virtually everyone already disbelieves in more than 99 percent of gods (Jupiter, Isis, Baal, the Golden Calf, Thor, etc.), and the atheist takes a short step further to disbelieve in 100 percent of gods.

It is true that in some matters a difference of one is irrelevant. One millimeter of pavement does not matter for a freeway. One eyelash fewer doesn't change our eye function. One molecule less of coffee in a cup goes unnoticed.

But shall we also argue that there is no important difference between being married and not being married, just one spouse further? Is there no important difference between having a baby and not having a baby, just one child further? I doubt anyone could escape criminal prosecution by pleading, "Officer, I only killed one person, and after all there is no significant difference between killing one person and killing no persons, so I should be released from custody." In some matters, the difference between one and none is enormously significant.

Sometimes, it may not be clear whether one fewer makes a difference. David Hume wrote: "How many languages are there, which you do not understand? The Punic, Spanish, Gallic, Egyptian, and so on. With regard to all these, you are as if you were deaf, yet you are indifferent about the matter. Is it then so great a misfortune to be deaf to one language more?"[3] Hume seems to imply a negative answer, but my answer to his question is that it is a great misfortune to be deaf to one language more. Most people who have lost their hearing seem to agree.

So, is the difference between atheism and theism like the difference between having one grain of salt or no grains of salt on a plate of French fries? Or is it more like having a baby or not having a baby?

Theist philosopher William Lane Craig remarked:

> If God does not exist, life is ultimately meaningless. If your life is doomed to end in death, then ultimately it does not matter how you live. In the end it makes no ultimate difference whether you existed or not. Sure, your life might have a relative significance in that you influenced others or affected the course of history. But ultimately mankind is doomed to perish in the heat death of the universe. Ultimately it makes no difference who you are or what you do. Your life is inconsequential. Thus, the contributions of the scientist to the advance of human knowledge, the research of the doctor to alleviate pain and suffering, the efforts of the diplomat to secure peace in the world, the sacrifices of good people everywhere to better the lot of the human race—ultimately all these come to nothing. Thus, if atheism is true, life is ultimately meaningless.[4]

But God's existence is not only a matter of significance in the ultimate end of things. According to the atheist philosopher Jean-Paul Sartre, God's existence is also a matter for meaning right here and now. In his *Existentialism and Human Emotions*, Sartre pointed out that if God does not exist, then we are "condemned to be free."[5] Life is without meaning and absurd not just ultimately but in our current situation.

Atheists themselves give ample evidence that the question of God's existence is a matter of significance. Why bother refuting a view if that view has no significance whatsoever? The efforts of atheists to show that there is no God is itself evidence that the question of God's existence is tremendously significant.

Moreover, atheists themselves implicitly acknowledge that there is an enormous difference between there being one God and there being no God. Otherwise, the "one God further" objection can be put on its head. If a difference of one is irrelevant, then atheists might as well accept just one God more and become theists. But all atheists (and all theists) think that there is a meaningful difference between theism and atheism. So the difference between one and none is a difference that matters to both atheists and theists.

But perhaps the "one God further" argument is best understood as a kind of inductive argument. We reject Hera, Baal, and Neptune, so we ought for similar reasons also to reject the God of Abraham. This way of construing the objection doesn't minimize the difference between theism and atheism but rather argues for the superior rationality of atheism as more consistent.

This seems to be the defense of the "one God further" objection advocated by psychology professor Geoffrey Miller, who tweeted, "If you don't believe in a god that hundreds of millions of other people do believe in, why don't you? Ask yourself honestly. From their point of view, you're an atheist."[6]

But if the Christian does not believe in Zeus, and the ancient pagan doesn't believe in Jesus, neither one of them is an atheist. An atheist believes that *no god at all exists*. The ancient pagan and the modern Christian both affirm a divine realm, although they disagree about the number of divine entities. It is foolishness, not consistency, to reject my mother as my mother, even though I reject all other women on earth as my mother.

If I ask myself honestly why I began to believe in God, the answer is that my parents talked and acted as if God existed. Other folks, raised by atheist parents, presumably began to believe in atheism because their parents talked and acted as if God did not exist. As we saw in chapter 6, the genetic fallacy indicates that the origin of a belief does not determine the truth of that belief. Being raised as a theist does not prove that atheism is true; being raised as an atheist does not prove that theism is true.

But perhaps Miller is inquiring not so much about how I *began* to believe that God exists, but rather why I *still* believe God exists. Having examined many arguments for and against God's existence, like other philosophers (Alvin Plantinga, Jennifer Frey, William Lane Craig, Eleonore Stump, and Edward Feser spring to mind), I've come to the conclusion that it is entirely reasonable to hold that God exists. Some believe in God because of the beauty, the order, and the intelligibility of a world that is caused. Others believe in God because of the improbability of a life-permitting universe, or the call of conscience, or the desire of the human person for perfect Truth, Goodness, and Love. None of these arguments points to the existence of a god like Zeus, Marduk, Odin, or any other finite entity. All of these arguments point to the existence of God as understood by Augustine of Hippo, Thomas Aquinas, and Edith Stein. If even one of these arguments is sound, then it is rational to reject the "one God further" objection.

15

Are There Many Gods?

The Five Ways and Polytheism

Even if we accept that there has to be an uncaused cause, why should we think that there's *only one* uncaused cause? Why couldn't there be two? After all, you were caused not only by your mother but also by your father. So maybe there are two uncaused causes, or maybe there are thirty-seven or ten million uncaused causes.

Moreover, why should we think that the Uncaused Cause is the same being as the Unmoved Mover? Indeed, maybe the five ways of Aquinas really prove five different gods. But if that's right, if Aquinas proves the truth of polytheism, then Aquinas's project of harmonizing faith and reason is going to be in real trouble. So, how do we move forward from here?

Well, let's think about what distinguishes one individual human being from another individual human being. What distinguishes you, for example, from me? One thing would be age. I doubt that we were born in the same year, month, day, hour, and minute. So one thing that probably distinguishes you and me is our age.

A second thing would be accidental characteristics like skin color. It is unlikely that we have exactly the same color skin. But even if we were born at exactly the same time and had exactly the same color skin, one thing that surely distinguishes you from me would be bodily location. I'm right here in this exact location. You're not right here right now. We're in different bodily locations.

We also have different origins. Unless my brother or sisters are reading this, I have one set of parents and you have another. And there are many accidental characteristics that I have that you lack. I'm wearing this particular shirt right now, and you are not wearing my shirt. And you have many accidental characteristics that I lack, such as the clothes you are wearing.

Any addition whatsoever to you that I don't have differentiates you from me. Likewise, any subtraction whatsoever from you that's not subtracted from me differentiates you and me. So we differ in lots of ways, but those last two categories of any addition whatsoever and any subtraction whatsoever you might say are catchalls.

So, let's imagine that there are two uncaused causes. Just as we are alike in being human, they are alike in being uncaused causes. What could distinguish one uncaused cause, X, from another uncaused cause, Y?

Could age differentiate them? If you're talking about an uncaused cause, you are talking about an eternal being, as we discussed in chapter 13. What does not have a beginning does not have a particular age. So, age cannot distinguish uncaused cause X from uncaused cause Y.

How about some accidental characteristic like skin color or hair length? Well, that wouldn't work either because an uncaused cause is a being that lacks all accidental characteristics, as we have explained in chapter 13. Only composed beings have accidental characteristics, and the uncaused cause cannot be composed. And so no accidental characteristic could differentiate uncaused cause X from uncaused cause Y.

How about bodily location? That's not going to work either because an uncaused cause is not composed. And if you're not composed, you can't be composed of bodily parts. But if you're not composed of bodily parts, well then you don't have a body. But if you don't have a body, you can't of course be in any particular bodily location. So we can't distinguish uncaused cause X from uncaused cause Y in terms of bodily location.

How about different parents? Well, we're talking about an *uncaused* cause. And if you're uncaused, you don't have parents.

How about some addition? Something is added to uncaused cause X that's not added to uncaused cause Y. But, as we have discussed in chapter 13, the uncaused cause is pure actuality, and if there's no potency, then there's no potency to have something added.

Well, how about some subtraction? Something is taken away from uncaused cause X that is not taken away from uncaused cause Y. Well, that's not going to work either. Just as some addition to an entity requires a potency in that entity, a subtraction also requires a potency. In other words, you can chop off my hand and subtract that from my body. But the reason that's possible is that I have the potency of having my hand chopped off. If I lacked that potency, you couldn't subtract that from me.

In sum, if you have a being that has no composition and therefore isn't composed of act and potency, there's no potency to lose anything. There's no potency for any subtraction whatsoever. And so, you can't distinguish uncaused cause X from uncaused cause Y by some subtraction.

The bottom line is this. If there is nothing that distinguishes uncaused cause X and uncaused cause Y, then they really are not two distinct things. They are in fact the very same thing. There is nothing at all, no addition, no subtraction, no time, no origin, no location that could distinguished uncaused cause X from uncaused cause Y. In other words, there can only be one Uncaused Cause.

The same reasoning applies to the idea that the Uncaused Cause and the Unmoved Mover are not the same being. If there is nothing that distinguishes the Uncaused Cause and Unmoved Mover, then they are not distinct in reality. They are in essence the very same thing. There is no time or age difference between the Uncaused Cause and Unmoved Mover, since they both must be eternal. There is no origin difference between the Uncaused Cause and Unmoved Mover since they are both without beginning. There can be no addition and no subtraction, since both have no potency to change. There can be no difference in bodily location between the Uncaused Cause and Unmoved Mover since pure actuality has no body and, therefore, no bodily location.

We should not confuse a difference in the words we use with a difference in reality. The commander-in-chief and the president of the United States are not two different people; these are two words used for the very same person. In a similar way, the Uncaused Cause and Unmoved Mover are not two different entities but two expressions used for the very same divine reality.

In *Summa Contra Gentiles*, Aquinas provides another argument from divine perfection that there can be only one God. Thomas says, "If then there are many Gods, there must be many perfect beings. But this is impossible. For if none of these perfect beings lacks some perfection and does not have any admixture of imperfection, which is demanded for an absolutely perfect being, nothing will be given in which to distinguish the perfect beings from one another."[1]

So the idea is something like this. If you have two perfect beings, they're alike in being perfect. Well, if they are to be *two* different beings, how do they differ? There's nothing you could add to one because if you added something to one, then the being in question would no longer be absolutely perfect.

And there's nothing that one or the other would lack in terms of perfection. Nothing that one or the other would have that detracts from perfection. Again, if they're absolutely perfect, they don't lack any perfection, and nothing further could be added to them. And so those two absolutely perfect beings in fact would not be different in any respect. But if there's nothing that distinguishes them in any respect, then they're not different beings at all.

A third argument Aquinas gives that there can be only one Uncaused Cause, who's the same as the Unmoved Mover, et cetera, is from Occam's razor, the principle that we should prefer the simplest explanation that accounts for all the effects. Imagine a crime scene, and the detective comes in and says, "Look. We can account for all the evidence we have in terms of a single killer. There's just one gun used, there's just one set of footprints leaving the crime scene, and there's just one extra set of DNA on the crime scene. In other words, all the available evidence can be accounted for by one killer."

In that scenario, it's superfluous and doesn't make any sense to posit that there are two or ten or twenty different killers. Similarly, we can account for all causality, all motion, all contingent being, all grades of perfection, and all order in the universe by one principle, by one God. And so it doesn't make sense to posit that there are multiple Gods.

The five ways to argue for God's existence are like five different kinds of evidence pointing to the same cause. Imagine a blind beggar who receives a donation. There might be five different kinds of evidence indicating that the same person gave the donation. The fingerprints point to one person giving this donation. The DNA left on the coin points to this individual giving the donation. Videographic evidence might show the individual giving the donation. Testimonial evidence of witnesses might confirm that this person gave the donation. And finally, the individual himself may say, "I gave the donation." In this way, five different kinds of evidence all point to the same cause. And so too, Aquinas argues that the five ways all point to the existence of just one God.

If Aquinas's reasoning is correct, there is one and only one God. This truth is also indicated through the faith of those who believe in the God of Abraham. Faith and reason are in harmony. Thomas has gone some way in establishing a reasonable faith and a faithful reason.

16

Is God like the Force in Star Wars?

Aquinas on God's Perfection

To answer the question, "Is God like the Force in *Star Wars*?" we need to first consider a different question, "Is God perfect?"

You might expect St. Thomas Aquinas to answer this question yes, but what he says is actually this: "God is *not* perfect in its original sense of the term."[1] The original meaning of the word *perfect* is "thoroughly made" (in Latin, *per factus*). If you think about a brand-new car, the car is perfect if it's made properly. If the directions of the engineers were followed and the manufacturing plant is working the way it should, you might say that the car comes out thoroughly made. It functions just the way it was designed to function.

But God of course can't be perfect in that sense. God, as the Uncaused Cause, is not thoroughly made—he isn't made at all. And so God is not perfect in that sense.

Is there any sense in which God is perfect? Well, yes. Thomas says, "By a certain extension of the name, perfect is said not only of that by which by way of becoming reaches a completed act, but also of that which, without any making whatever, is in complete act."[2] So, as we talked about in chapter 13, Aquinas thinks that God is complete act, unlimited actuality, maximal activity. And so God is perfect, not in the sense of being thoroughly made but in the sense of being complete, being maximal activity, being unrestricted actuality. Aquinas continues, "It is thus that, following the words of Matthew, we say that God is perfect: 'be perfect as your heavenly Father is perfect.'"[3]

Here we see a recurring theme for Aquinas, the harmony between faith and reason. Faith teaches us that God is perfect, and reason teaches us that God is perfect—but again, not perfect in the everyday sense of the term. Thomas advocates for a reasonable faith and a faithful reason.

Aquinas offers another argument from reason for God's kind of perfection. He says, "But just as every excellence and perfection is found in a thing according as that thing is, so every defect is found in it according as it is in some way not."[4] Evil is a lack of due perfection. This is true in both the physical order and the moral order. In the physical order, let's say that you have a broken leg. Your leg is obviously not what it should be; it is not perfect if it's broken. You might say that you're suffering or enduring an evil, that is, the evil of having a bad leg, a broken leg. A broken leg is lacking the perfection that it had before. The bones aren't in the proper place.

The same is true of a moral evil. A murderer is lacking in things that the killer ought to have: love for other people and just action toward other people. So, evil in the physical order—having a bad leg that is broken—and evil in the moral order—having a bad character—are alike. They both involve a lack of some perfection that an individual can and ought to have.

So, you might ask, is God the Uncaused Cause good? People of faith would say yes, and Aquinas thinks that we can come to the same conclusion using reason alone. If God is perfect, well, that which is perfect is good, and so God must be good. Aquinas teaches, "That which exists is good, and evil is a lack of existence. But of course God is the necessarily existing being."[5] So God has to be good. Let's break this down a bit more.

Aquinas says that "to be in act is for each being its good. But God is not only a being in act; He is His very act of being."[6] Evil, by contrast, is a lack of existence, a lack of due perfection. If you've got heart disease, your heart is lacking the kind of existence it should have. And if you've got a bad character, that means you're lacking the virtues you should have: justice, courage, temperance, practical wisdom.

By contrast, if you have the due perfection that you can and should have, well then, you're good. You don't have broken bones and a bad leg, but unbroken bones and a good leg. God has all that he should have. He is perfect, lacking no due perfection. And so, God is good. In fact, Aquinas holds that not only is God good, but God is goodness itself, the cause of all goodness.

So, is God like the Force in *Star Wars*? In *Star Wars*, the Force is partly good and partly bad, a mix of the light side and the dark side. So, is the Uncaused Cause like the Force? Well, that's another way of asking the question, can there be evil in God? Is God a combination of good and evil?

Well, as we explained in an earlier chapter, God is not composite. What is composite requires a prior composer. And if God is not composite, then God can't be a composite of partly good and partly evil. So, if God is good, and God is not composed, it follows that evil has no place in God.

Moreover, to be perfect is not to lack anything that is due. But evil is a lack of due perfection. We saw before how Aquinas argues that God is perfect. So, if his arguments are correct, if God is perfect and if it's true that evil is a lack of due perfection, then God can't be evil in any respect.

So, once again faith and reason are in harmony. Not only faith, but also reason teaches that God is entirely good, and that God is not a combination of partly good and partly evil. We have here a reasonable faith and a faithful reason.

17

Is God Intelligent?

On Divine Omniscience

In this chapter, I'd like to talk about a few different questions. Is God the Unmoved Mover, the Uncaused Cause, intelligent? If so, how does God understand? What does God understand?

So, is the Unmoved Mover intelligent? You might think that the Unmoved Mover is simply a force, a kind of first cause that doesn't know anything and can't know anything.

But recall from the previous chapter that Thomas Aquinas has argued that God enjoys all perfection. If Aquinas is right, if God has every perfection, and if it's true that intelligence is a perfection, then God must be intelligent. But is intelligence a perfection?

The agnostic skeptic John Stuart Mill certainly thought so. He wrote: "It is better to be a human being dissatisfied than a pig satisfied; better to be Socrates dissatisfied than a fool satisfied. And if the fool, or the pig, is of a different opinion, it is only because they only know their own side of the question."[1]

Isn't the loss of our own intelligence one of the worst things that could befall us? Do we not believe that Alzheimer's disease is one of the worst maladies? These insights point us to the conclusion that intelligence is a perfection. So, if Thomas's arguments are right, if God has every perfection, then God must be intelligent.

Thomas also provides another way that points to the same conclusion. In the fifth way to argue for God's existence, Thomas notes the order in the universe. There is an order found in nature, even in nonliving things. Consider the fact that force equals mass times acceleration. Or that hydrogen atoms interact in orderly ways with oxygen atoms to create water. Or that water itself freezes at a particular temperature, liquifies at another temperature, and evaporates at a third temperature. Scientific investigation reveals more and more the order of nature.

We need some explanation of this order. Imagine a book. The book has its pages in order. Even a particular page has ordered sentences. Each sentence has an order of subject and verb. We can justly infer that this book has an author. And to be an author is to be intelligent. For if an individual completely lacks intelligence, he or she cannot write one sentence, let alone a paragraph, let alone an entire book. So too, the book of nature requires an author, a first cause, who is intelligent.

This has become even more evident as scientific investigation has advanced. We know now that any life in the universe can exist only because the universe is "fine-tuned" to permit organic life. William Lane Craig notes, "To say that the universe is finely tuned means that the fundamental constants and quantities of nature fall into an extraordinarily narrow range of values that enable embodied, conscious observers to exist."[2] The fine-tuning of the universe points to an intelligent Creator. As Craig puts it:

> The argument from fine-tuning is a version of the argument for design that appeals not to biological examples of design, but to the initial conditions of the universe that are put in at the beginning of the universe in the Big Bang itself. And this argument can be simply summarized in three steps. Premise one: the fine-tuning of the universe for intelligent life is due to either physical necessity, chance, or design. Premise two is: it is not due to physical necessity or chance, and here you would present arguments to disqualify those two alternatives. Three: therefore, it is due to design. So, this argument, if successful, gives us a cosmic designer of the laws of nature and of the universe.[3]

So, if Aquinas is right or Craig is right, the Cause of time, space, and matter causes not only the existence of the universe but the order of the universe. God is not just a mover, but a mover who instills order in the universe. A mover who is imparting an order is aiming at something, aiming to create order.

If God is the first Unmoved Mover who orders things, God must be aiming to impart form, a plan, an order. But you can't apprehend a form, you can't have a plan, you can't seek to introduce order without intelligence. So, God the Uncaused Cause must be intelligent.

If any of these arguments is correct, then the Unmoved Mover, the First Cause, the Necessary Being must be intelligent.

But now a new problem arises. How can it be that God understands? If God is pure actuality, having no potency at all, then how can he also be intelligent? The idea that God is pure actuality seems to cause great problems for the idea that God is intelligent. We come to understand things by being open and receptive to them. If I want to understand what's written in a book, I've got to open the book up and read the letters there. My eyes have to be receptive to what's on the page. If I want to hear something from my friend, again, I have to listen to it. My ears have to be receptive to receiving the information. Whenever I learn something, my mind has to be receptive to receive something I didn't know before. When we learn things, we come to understand these things by being open and receptive. We learn by means of our potency. But God is absolutely perfect and fully actualized and doesn't have potency.

So, how can the Unmoved Mover move from not understanding to understanding? It seems that Thomas is caught in a dilemma. Either God is intelligent or God is not intelligent. If God is not intelligent, then Aquinas must be mistaken in his reasons for thinking God is intelligent. If God is intelligent, then Aquinas is wrong about God's nature as pure actuality. Maybe God in fact is a being like us, composed of act and potency. How does Aquinas get out of these difficulties?

Aquinas's answer to the question, "How does God understand?" is quite amazing. As you might expect, the way God understands is quite different from the way that human beings understand.

God is perfectly actualized, and so his understanding must also be perfectly actualized. We go from not knowing to knowing. We don't know a word of French, but then pick it up little by little. But God doesn't go from not knowing to knowing. God knows everything that he knows in a fully actualized way. God understands, Aquinas says, through nothing other than his essence.[4] By contrast, we begin to understand through our senses. I begin to understand things through seeing them, through hearing them, through tasting them. If God's understanding were through something other than his essence, then God would be in potency to that other thing. But as we saw before, God has no potency and so does not understand through anything other than his own essence.

So, in Thomas's view, God's knowledge and human knowledge are radically distinct. God understands all things at once. This can be challenging to understand, but an analogy might help.

When I first started to read, I sounded out each letter and then slowly put together a word. So I might sound out the sentence, "Pat hit the ball," and it would take me a while to figure out what sound the P makes, what sound the A makes, what sound the T makes. And then, it took a while longer to blend them all together. Finally, I'd get the word "Pat."

Once I became a better reader, I could read the whole word "Pat" all at once. I've taken a speed-reading course, so now I can read a short sentence like "Pat hit the ball" all at once. If I were a champion speed reader, I could read not just four words, but maybe ten words or twelve words or even more words all at once, all in one act of understanding. I would take it all in. So, imagine a super-powerful intellect that could read all the words of a book at once, in one act of understanding.

In Aquinas's view, God is something even beyond the super-powerful reader. God understands all things that are present to us, all things that are past to us, all things that are future to us, all in one eternal act of understanding. God doesn't *learn*; he simply knows.

And this is obviously very different from us. We understand one thing at a time. We understand this book, and then we put it down and pick up a different book, and then put that down and listen to our friend. Our understanding is sequential. God's knowledge also differs from ours in that it is not discursive. In human understanding, we can start from, say, the premise "all men are mortal" and the premise "Socrates is a man" and then conclude "Socrates is mortal." We move from one premise to the next. God's knowledge, by contrast, is direct and immediate.

And we also have habitual knowledge. We know many things that we are not thinking about at this moment. If someone asks me, "When was your mom born?" I go from not thinking about my mom's birthday to all of a sudden thinking about December 22. You have habitual knowledge of what your name is and where your toothbrush is. Presumably, you weren't thinking about either of those things until I mentioned them. You did know them in a sense, but you didn't know them actually; that is, you weren't currently thinking about them. You knew them only habitually.

God's knowledge is very different. God's knowledge is fully actual. God's knowledge is not habitual because habitual knowledge involves potentiality. You could think of the name of your best friend from eighth grade, and now you actually are thinking of that person.

This actual knowledge enables God to have a deeper relationship with us than any human person could have. We are always on God's mind. God is always thinking about us.

God also does not understand by composing and dividing, as we do. Sometimes we compose, we put two things together; for example, we think "all men" and we put that together with "are mortal." Sometimes we divide, and we say, "No man is twenty-five feet tall." God doesn't understand in that sort of way, by composing and dividing. God's understanding is in one eternal act that isn't brought about by composing and dividing, which, of course, are a multiplicity of acts.

Here's another question. What does God understand? Well, first of all, Aquinas says, God understands himself perfectly.[5] Why? Remember that God's understanding *is* God's essence. There's a perfect unity between God's mind and God's reality. Understanding is a unity of the one understanding and whatever is understood. So, if I understand you, that means there's some sort of unity between me, who's understanding, and you, the one who is understood. Understanding is a kind of unity between the mind and some reality.

God perfectly understands himself because there's a perfect unity between God's mind and God's essence. In fact, God's mind *is* God's essence; God's essence *is* God's mind.

Aquinas holds that God not only knows himself, but knows all other things in himself. An effect is known when its causes are known. And God knows himself, the cause of all that is caused. Therefore, he knows all the effects.

You might liken God to a mirror. If God looks in that mirror, God sees everything that is reflected in the mirror. Or you might liken God to an artist with self-knowledge. If an artist knows herself as an artist, she knows the art that she makes. If she had no idea about the art that she made, she could not know herself as an artist.

God is the First Cause, and he knows himself perfectly as a cause. But God couldn't know himself perfectly as a cause if he didn't know what he caused, the effects he brought about. God knows himself perfectly, so he knows himself as the First Cause perfectly. In knowing himself as First Cause, God knows all the effects that come from him. Hence, God knows everything that is caused: you, me, the fish of the sea, the blades of grass, and the buzzing of bees.

Moreover, God does not understand one thing, and then another thing, and then another thing. Rather, God has one eternal act of understanding. God, since he's not in time, doesn't understand one thing now and then some other thing later.

This leads to surprising insights. God understands you and understands your great-grandmother and understands your great-grandchild (if you'll have one) all at once, in one eternal act of understanding.

This depth of understanding allows God to relate to us in a richer way than any human person can relate to us. For people to love us deeply, they need a deep knowledge of us. Only if people know us well can they appreciate whatever is good in us, as well as our as-yet-unrealized potential for good. God's knowledge of us is perfect, so God can love us more than even our best friend on earth.

Faith and reason both point to the same conclusion. God knows the full truth about us. God knows every good deed we have ever done, and every good deed we will ever do. He sees the good intentions and all the noble ideals in our hearts. God sees the great potential we have to love others, to love ourselves, and to love him. What else can God do? We'll talk about that in our next chapter.

18

Does God Have a Will?

The Divine Will, the Human Will, Miracles, and Prayers

In previous chapters, we looked at reasons for thinking that some uncaused cause of the universe has to exist. We considered the way of remotion, by which we remove misunderstandings of who God is. And we also considered God's perfection and God's intelligence as distinct from human intelligence.

In this chapter, we will consider the divine will. First, do we have any good reasons to think that the Uncaused Cause has a will? In an earlier chapter, I talked about Aquinas's arguments for the existence of God. But one of the classic replies to Aquinas is to say, "Why in the world should we think that the Uncaused Cause is the same as the God of Abraham, the God of Isaac, the God of Jacob? The God of Abraham, Isaac, and Jacob has a will. He can choose to do things. An uncaused cause may exist, but it does not have a will."

Second, I want to look at the question of *how* God wills. Aquinas thinks that there are significant differences between a human will and the divine will. And so, we'll look at his understanding of how God wills.

Third, we'll consider the question, "Can God will a miracle?"

Finally, we'll consider another important objection to Thomas's view. If God knows everything, and if God does not change, aren't prayers of petition asking God to do something pointless?

Does the Uncaused Cause Have a Will?

It is clear that the God of the Bible has a will. Think about the stories where God wills to part the Red Sea, or God wills to send an angel to the Virgin Mary, or God wills to raise Jesus from the dead. All throughout the Bible, the God of the Bible wills to do various things.

So does the Uncaused Cause have a will? Aquinas's answer to this question is yes, the First Cause has to have a will. This truth is not a matter of faith alone, but of reason. Why does he think that God has a will? St. Thomas notes that an intellect does not cause except through a will. In other words, if all you did was think about something—simply think—that wouldn't cause anything in the external world. If all I did was think, I wouldn't make any changes to things outside of myself. And so an intellect doesn't cause such effects except through a will. An intellect alone doesn't cause unless a will is involved.

But Aquinas, as you know, thinks that the divine intellect *does* cause things. God is in fact the First Cause. If an intellect only causes things outside itself through a will, then it follows that the divine intellect has a will.

Aquinas provides another reason for thinking that the Unmoved Mover has a will, based on the fact that an intellectual being moves through the will. Think about an artist. The artist first thinks about how to paint the portrait, and then the artist moves beyond just thinking about painting to actually painting, to moving the paint onto the canvas. And this movement is caused by the will.

We know that Aquinas thinks that God does move things. Recall that Aquinas thinks that God is the Unmoved Mover. So if God is a mover, he's moving things via a will.

Moreover, it is a perfection to have a will. We would be much worse off if somehow we were to lose our freedom and become mindless robots doing what we do automatically. If Aquinas is right that God has every perfection, then God must have a will.

So, if any of these arguments is correct, the God of the philosophers, the Uncaused Cause, has a will. This means that the alleged "gap" between the God of the philosophers and the God of Abraham cannot rest on the idea that the God of the philosophers cannot will anything. Indeed, Thomas Aquinas thinks the Uncaused Cause is the God of Abraham, the God of Jesus. Reason and faith are in harmony.

How Does God Will?

Thomas thinks that God's will is radically different from ours. I have a will, but my will is not my essence. I can exist at times, for instance when I'm sleeping, without willing anything. And likewise, when I was a little baby, I was unable to freely will anything. I was a baby acting on instinct without free choice, and yet I existed. My will is therefore not my essence.

By contrast, God's will *is* his essence. What does it mean to say that God's will is his essence? God *is* his own will, just as God *is* his own understanding. God's will and God's essence are one. It's not as if there's God's essence, and then in addition to that, as something combined, there is also God's will. Rather, God's will is identical with his essence. By contrast, in all human beings, their essence is distinct from their acts of willing.

If the divine essence existed, and then the divine will was added to it, then of course God would be composed. You'd have what God is substantially, and then in addition to that, there'd be what God is accidentally. But God is not composed, for what is composed requires a composer prior to what is composed. So, God cannot be composed of what God is essentially and what God is accidentally. By contrast, substantially, I'm a human being, and then accidentally, I might will this or I might will that.

Remember also that Aquinas concluded that God's intellect is the same as his essence. If God's intellect *is* his essence, and God's *will* is his essence, that means God's intellect is the same as his will, and vice versa. So when God acts, he doesn't first know something and then will it, as we do. Instead, his act of knowing and his act of willing are the same—and both are God himself, because God is pure act.

Let's continue thinking about the question of *how* God wills.

Consider multitasking. How many things can you do at once? Well, I don't know about you, but I can only do a few things at once. I can walk, and I can snap my fingers, and I can at the same time hum a song, and I can close one eye. So I can consciously do maybe four or five things at once.

St. Thomas thinks that God is different. God has just one eternal act of the will. In that one eternal act of the will, God wills everything that he wills. So, in one eternal act of the will, God creates the material universe and time. In one eternal act of the will, God also creates human beings. In one eternal act of the will, God also invites Abraham to leave his homeland. In one eternal act of the will, God also invites Moses to lead the people out of Egypt. In one eternal act of the will, God also invites a virgin named Mary to be the mother of Jesus. And God also invites each of us right now to love him in return.

So God, you might say, is the ultimate multitasker. But it would be better to say that God is the ultimate unitasker. God does everything he does in one eternal act of the will. Everything that to us is from the very beginning of time, to the present, to the future, is done by God in this one eternal act of the will. God's will is very different from ours.

God doesn't go from potentially willing something to actually willing something. That's what you and I do. We could potentially eat a sandwich, and then maybe we choose to actually eat the sandwich. But God, Aquinas thinks, is different. God is not a being who's composed of act and potency. And so God doesn't go from potentially willing something to actually willing something. What God does is everything, God wills everything in just one eternal act. And part of that will is to will that different aspects of his will unfold in time.

You might think about God's one eternal act of the will as a little bit like the last will and testimony of a rich woman—let's call her Jennifer. Jennifer is worried that if her son George inherits all of her money at once, he will go to Las Vegas and blow it on partying and gambling. So, Jennifer makes her will. In the will, Jennifer designates that when George turns thirty, he gets a small percentage of his inheritance. When George turns forty, he gets a little more. Finally, when George turns fifty, he gets the rest of his inheritance. Hopefully, at fifty years old, George is not going to go to Vegas and blow it all on the roulette wheel. Jennifer has just one will, but that one will unfolds in time.

God, in one eternal act of the will, wills everything that to us is past, present, and future. And part of what God wills, at least according to Aquinas, is our own individual existence. Aquinas thinks that each one of us is willed intentionally and individually by God. Obviously, our mother and father were involved in our coming into existence. Aquinas thinks that the mother and father combine to provide the *material cause* of a child, but that God provides the *formal cause* of the child, the soul. And so each one of us is made not only by our mother, not only by our father, but also by God, who gives us our immortal soul.

What God knows includes us. And it's not as if God isn't thinking about us sometimes, and then maybe we pray, and God starts thinking about us. Aquinas holds that God is always thinking about us and therefore is always available to relate to us. Likewise, God is always willing our good. As long as we exist, God is willing our continued existence, our life.

God's one eternal act of the will includes not only creating us, not only holding us in existence, but also inviting us to love him in return.

Let's consider our third question.

Can God Will Miracles?

Can the Uncaused Cause will miracles? The God of Abraham and of Jesus, the God of scripture, clearly wills miracles. God parts the Red Sea so the Hebrews can escape the Egyptians, the Virgin Mary conceives a baby by the power of the Holy Spirit, and Jesus rises from the dead. There are many, many other miracles in scripture. So, another question I'd like to consider is, "Can the Uncaused Cause will a miracle?"

Let's consider an *a fortiori* argument, the argument from the stronger. The idea is something like this. If you have a weight lifter who can lift five hundred pounds over his head, then that weightlifter can also lift one hundred pounds over his head. Put another way, if an Olympian can high-jump over seven feet, then that Olympian can high-jump over five feet. If I can do what requires more strength, I can do what requires less strength. That's an argument *a fortiori.*

If someone is powerful enough to bring about the greater thing, then they are powerful enough to bring about the lesser thing. So if God is powerful enough to *create* the order of nature out of nothing, then God is powerful enough to *change* the order of nature. If God is powerful enough to make all time, all space, and all matter from nothing, then God is powerful enough to make the Virgin Mary have a baby. If God is powerful enough to make all time, all space, and all matter out of nothing, then God is powerful enough to make Jesus rise from the dead. In Aquinas's view, God is indeed powerful enough to make all time, all space, and all matter out of nothing. And so, God is powerful enough to change the order of nature and to cause miracles.

Can God's Will Change?

Finally, let's address the topic of petitionary prayer. If God is pure actuality with no potency, then does it make sense to ask God to do anything? In the Our Father, Jesus taught his disciples to pray "give us this day our daily bread." But if God is pure actuality, his mind is unchanging and his will is unchanging. And if God's will is unchanging, then it seems that any prayer of petition—like "God, please cure my friend's disease"—makes no sense. Either God from all eternity wills to heal the friend or he does not.

If God wills from all eternity to heal the friend, then it seems the prayer makes no difference. God would have done it anyway.

If God from all eternity wills not to heal the friend, then it also seems the prayer makes no difference, because God's will is not changed by the prayer. Either way, prayer of petition seems not to make any difference.

Now, how would Aquinas respond to this problem? If God knows all things, then God knows from all eternity whether or not you will pray. God can then from all eternity take this prayer into account. God knows in his eternal knowledge that I'm going to pray, "Give us this day our daily bread." God knows from the very beginning that I'm going to pray that this person gets healed. God can then will from all eternity to do certain things because he knows that we pray for them, and God wills to grant our prayer.

Now, why would God do this? Well, if it's true that God wants to be in a relationship with us, if it's true that God wants each of us to be a particular kind of person, then he might arrange the universe so that we are granted certain things that we pray for.

Parents do something similar. Sometimes, when my kids were little, I would decide beforehand to give my children ice cream *if and only if* the children said, "please." If Cate came up to me and said, "Give me the ice cream, Dad," I would say no. On the other hand, if she came up to me and said, "Please, can I have a bowl of ice cream?" I would say yes. I had decided before she even asked that I would give her the ice cream if she asked politely.

Now, why did I do that? I did that because I aimed to raise kids that were courteous and polite. I thought it was good for them to be courteous and polite people for their own sakes and the sake of others.

In a similar way, God wants to have a loving relationship with us. God wants to encourage us to turn to him in times of need. God wants to encourage us to pray. And so God wills from all eternity to grant certain things on condition that we pray for them.

But, sometimes we might pray for something and what we pray for does not come to pass. The same thing was true when my kids asked for ice cream. Would I give my kids ice cream every single time they asked for it, so long as they said please? Well, no.

Sometimes my kids might ask for ice cream immediately before dinner. Despite their saying please, I'd say, "No, I'm not going to give you ice cream right now because we're about to eat dinner. And if you just eat ice cream, you won't get all the healthy nutrients that you're going to get from dinner."

So just as a parent sometimes knows better than a child whether or not to grant a petition, so too, in Aquinas's view, God knows better than human beings what things to grant and what things not to grant when we pray for them. In sum, faith and reason work together in terms of petitionary prayer.

19

Can God Destroy Himself?

On Divine Omnipotence

When I was a kid at Camp Nor'wester in the San Juan Islands of the Pacific Northwest, I read a question written in a bathroom stall: "Can God make a rock that he cannot lift?" It seemed to be an unsolvable dilemma. I thought, well, if God can make a rock that he can't lift, then something is more powerful, greater than God. But St. Anselm of Canterbury taught that "God is that than which nothing greater can be conceived."[1] So, God cannot make a rock he cannot lift. On the other hand, I thought, if God cannot make a rock he can't lift, then God is not omnipotent. He's not all-powerful. I was really confused. It got me thinking, and I thought about that question for a long time, and I couldn't figure out an answer.

A similar puzzle arises from thinking about the idea of divine destruction. Can God destroy himself? In an earlier chapter, we saw how Aquinas provided good reasons for thinking that God is eternal. But if God *can* destroy himself, then he's not eternal, existing without limit of a beginning or an end. On the other hand, if God *cannot* destroy himself, then there are some things God cannot do. God is not really omnipotent. This question, "Can God destroy himself?" seems to lead to problems either with God being eternal or with God being omnipotent.

Richard Dawkins poses another philosophical dilemma. Dawkins argues that these traditional attributes are mutually incompatible. "If God is omniscient, he must already know how he is going to intervene to change the course of history using his omnipotence. But that means he can't change his mind about his intervention, which means he is not omnipotent."[2] In Dawkins's view, the idea of God is like a square circle or a triangle with four sides—contradictory and therefore absurd and impossible. If God is unchanging, he cannot change his mind. But if God cannot do something (such as change his mind), God cannot be all-powerful.

I only found out years later that Thomas Aquinas provides principles that allow us to think about these questions. If God wills something other than himself, he wills it with necessity of supposition, a kind of necessity that arises *if* some other condition is present. For example, if Socrates is running, then by necessity of supposition, his legs are moving. If there are human beings, then by necessity of supposition, there are rational animals. Can God will that a human being not be a rational animal? Can God will that Socrates run and that Socrates's legs not be moving?

No. If God wills something, then God would be contradicting himself if he also willed something contrary to what he wills. So, if he wills that human beings are free, then God would contradict himself if he also willed that human beings not be free at the same time and in the same respect.

It's not as if there's a logic book that is above God that determines what God can and cannot do. It's rather that God does not contradict himself. God doesn't will that this human being is free, and at the same time, and in the same respect, also will that this human being not be free.

As human beings, of course, we can contradict ourselves, and we do contradict ourselves as we talked about in the first chapter of this book. But Aquinas thinks that this is not something that can happen for God. To be in self-contradiction is to be unwise and irrational. But God is not unwise or irrational, so God does not contradict himself.

Why do we contradict ourselves? Well, we can actually locate the source of some of our contradictions within our own brains. I will to be healthy, so I will to eat healthy food. I can also will what is pleasurable, so I can will to eat unhealthy food. There is part of my brain, the prefrontal cortex, that acts in a rational way, and that part of me wills to be healthy. But there's another part of my brain, the limbic cortex, that wants to eat fatty, salty, unhealthy food. One reason that I can contradict myself is that part of me can be set against another part of me, the rational prefrontal cortex part of myself against the limbic cortex part of myself.

But as was explained in chapter 13, in God there are no parts. God is not a being who is composed. And if God has no parts, then part of God can never be in conflict with another part of God.

As explained earlier, the First Cause is not composed, for what is composed requires a prior composer. So, God's will cannot be set in opposition to another part of the divine will. If the First Cause has no parts, God cannot be set in opposition to another part of God, so the divine will could never come into conflict with another part of the divine will.

Aquinas provides another reason that God cannot will the impossible. He says that the will is of the understood good. But the impossible cannot be understood, and so cannot be an understood good. Let me try to explain this. Before we will anything, we have to first understand it as a possibility. If I will to go get a glass of water, I have to understand that there's a good out there, namely water, that I could get. Before we will anything, we first must understand it as a possibility, and it must be something that's understood as good. But what is impossible cannot be understood, and so it cannot be an understood good.

We can't understand the reality of a square circle. It's not a possible reality we can know. We can say the words "square circle," but we cannot have our mind united to the reality of a square circle. It's not a possible object of knowledge. If a square circle cannot be understood as a reality, it cannot be an understood good. But if it can't be an understood good, it can't be the object of the will. And so God can't will what is impossible.

C. S. Lewis put the point this way:

> [God's] omnipotence means power to do all that is intrinsically possible, not to do the intrinsically impossible. You may attribute miracles to Him, but not nonsense. This is no limit to His power. If you choose to say "God can give a creature free will and at the same time withhold free will from it," you have not succeeded in saying *anything* about God: meaningless combinations of words do not suddenly acquire meaning simply because we prefix them with the two other words "God can." It remains true that all *things* are possible with God: the intrinsic impossibilities are not things but nonentities.[3]

For God to will the impossible would be for the divine will to be set against the divine will and against the divine understanding. But part of God cannot be set against another part of God, for God is not composed of parts.

How does this understanding of God help us to answer the questions posed earlier? Can God make a rock that he cannot lift? No. God cannot make a rock that he can't lift. If God could make a rock that he couldn't lift, that rock would be greater than God in some respect. But it's impossible that anything could be greater than God. And so, it's impossible to make a rock that's greater than God in any respect.

And what about the question, "Can God destroy himself?" Well, if God could destroy himself, then God would not be eternal. To be eternal means that it is impossible to go out of existence. And, for reasons we explained in an earlier chapter, God is eternal. God is not composed, so God cannot be decomposed and die. God can't destroy himself.

God's will *is* omnipotent. And to be omnipotent means to be *omni-*, namely all, *potent*, that is, able to do all possible things. But divine destruction is not possible. That's something that can't be.

And what about the argument of Dawkins? Recall that he objected, "If God is omniscient, he must already know how he is going to intervene to change the course of history using his omnipotence. But that means he can't change his mind about his intervention, which means he is not omnipotent."[4]

Is Dawkins correct that omnipotence and immutability are mutually exclusive? It is true that we can do things that God cannot do. For example, we can kill ourselves, we can be deceived, and we can get injured. God cannot die, cannot be deceived, and cannot be injured. However, that God cannot do such things does not mean that God is not all-powerful, because the potential to die, to be in error, and to be injured really indicates not a perfection but a lack of perfection, not power but a lack of full power. Is changing your mind a power and a perfection or a lack of power and an imperfection? If you do not know something and you change your mind to knowing it, such a change makes you more perfect. But in Thomas's view, God already knows everything. So if God were to change with respect to knowledge, it would not be a manifestation of perfection but a falling away from perfect knowledge. Therefore, omniscience and immutability are not self-contradictory, but rather different characteristics that necessarily belong to the First Cause we call God.

Dawkins also mistakenly assumes that both omniscience and omnipotence would be at work in time. For Thomas, God doesn't "already" know how he is "going to" intervene. God is eternally intervening and is eternally knowing his intervention at all points in history.

Likewise, God can't, for instance, not know himself. God *must* know himself because he *is* his own knowledge. Now, I can get amnesia, but that reflects the weakness of vulnerable human nature. I'm not an omnipotent being. And in a similar way, the fact that God must know himself reflects something of the greatness of God. God cannot be ignorant. I could get Alzheimer's disease and not know who I am, but that kind of thing cannot happen to God.

So God can do all *possible* things. But some things are *not* possible, like a square circle, or like God not knowing himself, or like God destroying himself.

To conclude this chapter, let us consider God and emotions. Our emotions take place through bodily changes. For example, when you are angry, your heart beats faster and adrenaline shoots through your body. When you cease being angry, your body changes back to its resting state.

But if Aquinas is right that God is not composed and has no body, then God can't have bodily changes. If emotions necessarily involve bodily changes, then God doesn't have emotions. If God is perfectly actualized, then God can't go from one state to some other state. So, God can't have emotional changes that are typical of human beings. God cannot become sad or angry.

These views pose a problem in a way for Aquinas. Scripture, for instance, explicitly says, "The anger of the Lord was kindled against Israel" (2 Kgs 13:3). The Bible seems to teach that God became angry. So how does Aquinas deal with those kinds of passages from the Bible? It seems as if Aquinas's reason, saying that God has no emotions, is in contradiction to revelation. Maybe faith and reason are opposed after all.

But Aquinas notes that there are other passages in scripture that talk about God being unchanging. "For I the Lord do not change; therefore you, O sons of Jacob, are not consumed" (Mal 3:6). The Epistle of James teaches, "Every good endowment and every perfect gift is from above, coming down from the Father of lights with whom there is no variation or shadow due to change" (1:17).

Is this a contradiction? No. Aquinas thinks both kinds of biblical passages are true, provided they are interpreted properly. This may be explained by analogy.

Think about the sun. The sun is hot, giving off light. Now, that won't always be true. Several billion years from now, the sun is going to burn out. But in terms of our human existence, you could say that the sun is always hot, the sun is always bright, the sun is unchangingly active in heating and brightening.

But *our experience* of the sun is something that does change. Imagine a relaxing Fourth of July day. You're sitting beside the pool enjoying a nice cool drink. It feels wonderful that the sun is really hot. It's 90 degrees, and every time you get a little bit too hot, you jump in the pool and cool off. Then you get out of the pool again. You might say you experience the sun as loving you.

On the other hand, imagine the very same day, the very same sun. But rather than sitting beside the pool and jumping in the water every now and then, you are walking through a desert. The sun is blazing down on you, and you're worried about getting dehydrated. You feel as if you might even die of heat exhaustion. You might say you are experiencing the sun as if it were an enemy hating you.

Now, there's no difference whatsoever in the sun. The sun is always doing what the sun is always doing. But what has changed is you. You went from one circumstance, one relationship to the sun, sitting beside the pool and jumping in the cool water, to a radically different relationship to the sun, walking through the desert and feeling like you're about to die.

So, in a similar way, Thomas holds that God is always doing what God is always doing. God is always loving. God is always knowing. God is willing the good. If we're in harmony with God—if we're willing what is good, if we're loving others—then we're going to enjoy harmony with God. We will experience that harmony as something very positive.

On the other hand, we may not be in harmony with God. If we're acting against love, if we're acting against the truth, if we're acting against goodness, well, we're going to experience God in a different way. We may experience God as alien to us, as something foreign to us, as something judgmental of us. We're going to be like the person walking in the desert in the blazing sun. But it's not *God* who's changing. What can change and does change radically is our relationship with God.

So, the scriptural passages that talk about God "becoming angry" are accurately portraying the disharmony between people and God. When people are out of harmony with God, they experience God as if he were angry. St. Thomas is making the point that we misread scripture if we read it as a literal sense of anger. We'd be mistaken if we thought God has a body, and God's heart rate goes up, and God gets a lot of adrenaline because he becomes really angry. God is always loving, but we don't always enjoy that love.

20

Is God Love?

On Divine Omnibenevolence

We've talked about a lot of important questions. Does God the Uncaused Cause exist? Could there be more than one Uncaused Cause? How can we contrast human knowledge and divine knowledge, human will and divine will? Are faith and reason in harmony? But now we come to perhaps the most important idea about God.

Many people have heard the idea that God is love. Can we know this not just from revelation, but also from reason, on the basis of philosophy?

"God is love." What does this mean? We can think about love in two different ways. On the one hand, we can think about love as an emotion, something that happens to us. We "fall" in love in an emotion that we do not control. On the other hand, love can also be considered as a choice, a decision, or activity.

Now, for reasons explained in the previous chapter, God doesn't have emotions as bodily changes. God is not composed of parts making up a body. And so, love as an emotion involving bodily change is, for Aquinas, something that God does not have. But God does, on the other hand, have loving activity. God has a will. And so, love as a choice, as a decision, is something that God does.

Thomas thinks that love as an action is made up of three different aspects. One is willing the good of the other person for the other person's sake. If I love my daughter, I choose to do good rather than evil to her. I try to help her learn, have friends, and flourish rather than hurt her. The second is that love also involves appreciating the other person. When I love my daughter, I appreciate the good that is in her. I appreciate how intelligent she is, and how she does her homework right away, and how beautiful she is, and what a sweet person she is. I appreciate the good that is in her. And finally, love involves seeking unity with the other person. I seek unity with my daughter by spending time with her, singing songs with her, going out to eat with her.

Love is a choice. It's a choice to will the good of the other person, it's a choice to appreciate the other person, and it is a choice to seek unity with the other person.

In chapter 91 of the first part of the *Summa Contra Gentiles*, Aquinas gives a number of philosophical arguments that God is love. Aquinas maintains that not just faith but also philosophy can lead us to the conclusion that "God is love." Here's why he thinks that.

The nature of love is to will the good for the one we love. God wills our existence and wills that we have good things, like friends, health, knowledge, for our own sake. Remember that Aquinas thinks that God is absolutely perfect. God can't be improved. God has every good. So when God wills *our* good, it's not so he can improve. God doesn't need anything from us. And so when God wills our good, this is willing our good for our own sake. But that's exactly what true love is.

Moreover, God also appreciates the good that is in us. Think about all the good things you've done throughout your life. That's a lot. If I think back to my own life, I'm sure I've forgotten all kinds of good things I've done. I'm sure at some point in first grade I was nice to someone on the playground, but I've forgotten about that.

God knows, in Aquinas's view, all the good that we've done all through our life, from the very beginning of our life as little kids all the way through to the present hour. God knows that, and God appreciates that. If you love someone, you know and appreciate the good that they are, the good that they have, the good that they've done. God knows and appreciates those goods in us.

Aquinas also links up love with unity. He holds that the more the lover is one with the one he loves, the more intense is the love.[1] Think about the great intensity of love that can exist between a husband and wife. Why can their love be so intense? Because their love has deep multidimensional unity. They're unified in raising their children, they're unified in living their lives together, they're unified in a bodily way. They can have a very intense unity, and therefore, they can have a very intense love.

But God's love for us is even more intense. God is with us every minute of every day. He is always ready to communicate with us. He knows us better than anyone. He is unified with us more than any human being could be. For this reason, Greg Bottaro suggests we pray, "Ever-present God, here with me now, help me to be here with you."[2]

What is the point of all this discussion of God? Well, Aquinas thinks that knowing these truths about God does more than simply satisfy our intellectual curiosity. In order to love something, we have to know something about it. If we're going to love our best friend, we have to know our best friend. If you know your best friend and your best friend is an amazing person, your love for your friend is going to intensify as you learn more about the goodness of your friend. Your love is going to intensify because your knowledge is greater.

If the object of our love is lovable and good, then our love for that object intensifies as we gain greater knowledge of that object. That's exactly why Aquinas wrote what he wrote. St. Thomas wanted us to know God more and therefore love God more. But if God wants us to know him and love him, then why does it often seem that God is absent, especially in the face of suffering? Why isn't God's existence more obvious? To that topic we now turn.

21

Why Isn't God's Existence Obvious?

Divine Hiddenness and Seeking Signs

In the movie *The Man with Two Brains*, Steve Martin plays a widower who is considering getting remarried. His beautiful but greedy girlfriend Dolores artfully conceals her cruelty. One day Martin stands before a portrait of his dead first wife, Rebecca, and begs, "Rebecca, if there is anything wrong with my feelings for Dolores, just give me a sign." Immediately, lights blink, winds whip, and an earthquake erupts. The portrait spins in circles on the wall, and Rebecca's voice from beyond the grave cries out louder and louder, "No! Noo! Nooo!" And then, after fifteen seconds or so, it all stops. Martin, disheveled by the winds, looks at the off-kilter portrait and says, "Just any kind of sign. I'll keep on the lookout for it."

In *Existentialism Is a Humanism*, Jean-Paul Sartre noted, "It is I myself, in every case, who have to interpret the signs."[1] This insight holds true also when looking for signs from God. If spectacular golden letters appeared in the sky spelling out, "I AM the God of Abraham; believe in ME," would this sign bring people to a relationship with God? Golden letters in the sky wouldn't exactly prove that *God* exists because presumably a powerful alien or even a swarm of drones could make those letters appear in the sky. The atheist philosopher A. J. Ayer had a near death experience and wrote, "I was confronted by a red light, exceedingly bright, and also very painful even when I turned away from it. I was aware that this light was responsible for the government of the universe."[2] But this sign did not dislodge his atheism. Why not?

In his poem "London," William Blake wrote of "mind-forg'd manacles." As Peter Harrison pointed out in his book *Some New World: Myths of Supernatural Belief in a Secular Age*: "What we 'see' is thus at least partly determined by what we already believe. This is not completely removed from Anselm's 'faith seeking understanding' and goes some way towards recounting how the same event might be interpreted in ways that are consistent with both naturalism and non-naturalism." So, it is not the case that "the supernatural is no longer directly experienced, but rather that what we experience is no longer labelled 'supernatural.'"[3]

Scientists call this predictive processing. What we believe, what we think, what we seek, shapes what we see. In the online video "The Monkey Business Illusion,"[4] people are asked to count how many times players wearing white shirts pass a basketball as they move among players wearing black shirts passing another basketball. In the midst of all this action, a person wearing a gorilla costume walks through the players. About half of the people watching the video don't see the gorilla. We can have eyes but not see.

Moreover, if Jews, Christians, and Muslims are right, God is a spiritual being, not a material object like a gorilla. We cannot see God as we see molecules under a microscope or stars in the night sky.

Indeed, the hiddenness of God is itself a biblical teaching. Isaiah says, "Truly, you are a God who hide yourself" (45:15). God hides his face from Moses, saying, "you cannot see my face; for man shall not see me and live" (Ex 33:20).

But although hidden from direct sight, Christians believe God does disclose himself. As Fr. Kevin Grove puts it, "God's revelation is often enough discoverable under the meekest sign of its opposite."[5] The helpless baby born in a stable to a mother without means is really a king. The convicted criminal dying on a cross is actually the ultimate judge and Lord of life. God is hidden in the sacraments, hidden in the scriptures, and hidden in the discouraged, the bedraggled, and the addicted. As Gerard Manley Hopkins wrote, "The world is charged with the grandeur of God." St. Ignatius of Loyola found God in all things.

According to St. Thomas Aquinas, the hiddenness of God does not last forever. Those in heaven *do* see God face-to-face. Seeing God is enjoying eternal happiness. Why is this vision of God reserved for the life to come?

In chapter 8 of *The Screwtape Letters*, C. S. Lewis points out that if God were to make himself "Irresistible and Indisputable," this would override the human ability to choose whether to love. If we are to be free to choose to love or not to love God, then God cannot appear to us face-to-face in overwhelming power and majesty. For this reason, God chooses to woo, not compel, to be delicate rather than overwhelming.

Jesus suggested that miraculous signs have limited value in bringing people to God: "If they do not hear Moses and the prophets, neither will they be convinced if some one should rise from the dead" (Lk 16:31). Maybe we find God, if we find God at all, in everyday life. Maybe, if you have been looking for a sign to seek God, this is it.

In the next four chapters, we will consider the most important objection to God's existence: the apparent contradiction between the existence of an all-powerful, all-good God and the fact of suffering and evil.

22

Can Evil Be a Means to the Good?

The Story of the Chinese Farmer

Long ago, there was a widowed Chinese farmer. The farmer and his only son labored through the cold winds of winter and scorching rays of summer with their last remaining horse. One day, the son didn't lock the gate of the stable properly, and the horse bolted away.

When neighbors learned what happened, they came to the farmer and said, "What a sadness this is! Without your horse, you'll be unable to maintain the farm. What a failure that your son did not lock the gate properly! This is a great tragedy!"

The farmer replied, "Maybe yes, maybe no."

The next day, the missing horse returned to the farmer's stable, bringing along with it six wild horses. The farmer's son locked the gate of the stable firmly behind all seven horses.

When neighbors learned what happened, they came to the farmer and said, "What happiness this brings! With seven horses, you'll be able to maintain the farm with three of them and sell the rest for huge profits. What a blessing!"

The farmer replied, "Maybe yes, maybe no."

The next day, the farmer's son was breaking in one of the wild horses. The son got thrown from the horse, fell hard on rocks, and broke his leg.

When neighbors learned what had happened, they came to the farmer and said, "What a great sadness this is! Now, you'll be unable to count on your son's help. What a shame to have broken his leg! What a tragedy!"

The farmer replied, "Maybe yes, maybe no."

The next day, a general from the Imperial Chinese Army arrived to conscript all the young men of the village into the army. Their assignment was to fight on the front lines of a battle against a terrifying enemy of overwhelming force. The farmer's son, because of his broken leg, was not taken.

When neighbors learned what happened, they came to the farmer and said, "What a great joy! Your son avoided facing certain death on the front lines of the battle. What a blessing!"

The farmer replied, "Maybe yes, maybe no."

What does this story mean? The story of the Chinese farmer teaches us vital lessons about the problem of evil.

The story teaches us to suspend judgment about what appears to be a tragedy or a triumph. Can we really always tell what is fortunate and what is unlucky? Sometimes, the wiser course of action is to withhold judgment rather than definitively declare what happens as good or bad.

A Stoic philosopher like Epictetus would see the story as portraying the farmer's rightful detachment from what is not in his control, matters about which he should be indifferent. In his *Enchiridion*, Epictetus taught, "There are things which are within our power, and there are things which are beyond our power. Within our power are opinion, aim, desire, aversion, and, in one word, whatever affairs are our own. Beyond our power are body, property, reputation, office, and, in one word, whatever are not properly our own affairs."[1] Losing his horse, gaining new horses, his son's broken leg, and his son's avoiding deadly combat are all matters that were not within the farmer's power to control. In this Stoic view, the farmer is wise in not letting these external matters disturb him. As First Lady Martha Washington said, "I am still determined to be cheerful and to be happy in whatever situation

I may be, for I have also learned from experience that the greater part of our happiness or misery depends upon our dispositions, and not upon our circumstances; we carry the seeds of the one or the other about with us, in our minds, wherever we go."[2] The farmer seems to have what is asked for in the Serenity Prayer: "God, grant me the serenity to accept the things I cannot change, the courage to change the things I can, and the wisdom to know the difference."

The story teaches us that what appears to be bad initially may ultimately be a blessing. Our immediate vision is not always 20/20. How often has something that seemed like a major setback, or even a tragedy, turn out to be the beginning of something great? Do we not often see only in hindsight that a difficulty was just what we needed to grow and flourish in the long term? Painful and challenging experiences often lead to development, especially when reframed as opportunities to learn to grow in skills, in virtues, and in bonds. The ancient Greek playwright Aeschylus said: "He who learns must suffer. And even in our sleep pain that cannot forget falls drop by drop upon the heart, and in our own despair, against our will, comes wisdom to us by the awful grace of God."[3] Terrible suffering is a medicine so dangerous that it may only be rightfully employed by the Divine Physician.

The story of the Chinese farmer also teaches us about the complicated relationship between suffering and well-being. Sometimes what is indeed bad (breaking a leg) can lead to something good (avoiding death in battle). And yet what is bad remains bad, even if something good comes from it. It is always bad when an attempted murder takes place. Yet, in some cases, an attempted murder leads to something good, such as a serial killer finally getting arrested. Similarly, what is good remains good, even if something bad comes from it. It is good for a husband and wife to have a child, even if years later it is bad that the child becomes a criminal.

Moreover, the story of the Chinese farmer teaches us something about what we ultimately consider good and evil amid the vicissitudes of the lesser goods and evils in life. For people of faith, the ultimate good is enjoying perfect Love, perfect Goodness, and perfect Beauty forever. This is called heaven, the community of all those who love each other and God perfectly. The ultimate evil is eternal self-willed loneliness, a heart forever divided against itself, a will ever frustrated in seeking the good. In the *Inferno*, Dante imagined the fate of the worst lost souls in the lowest circle of hell. They are in the coldest and smallest prison cell imaginable, totally encapsulated in ice, isolated from each other, and lacking in even the smallest freedom. The ice is made by Satan, who cries tears of frustration as he flaps his great wings struggling in vain to free himself from the ice. Satan's vain, tearful struggle against God only creates more and more ice, increasing his imprisonment.

The great French novelist Léon Bloy once wrote, "The only real sadness, the only real failure, the only great tragedy in life, is not to become a saint."[4] If so, then the only perfect happiness, the only ultimate success, the greatest blessing in life, is to become a saint. Someday, will you and I enjoy the perfect happiness of the saints? Maybe yes, maybe no.

23

Does Any Evil Disprove God's Existence?

The Logical Problem of Evil

The argument from evil is the most powerful reason to deny the existence of God. It comes in two versions. The first version is the logical problem of evil, and the second version is the evidential problem of evil. In this chapter, we will explore the first version. The logical problem of evil holds that any evil whatsoever disproves God's existence. If there is just one person with a painful hangover, this suffering is enough to indicate that God does not exist. No need for abstract speculation; too many wine coolers at a Prince concert is all you need to disprove the existence of the Almighty.

What is the argument for this view? The ancient Greek philosopher Epictetus put the argument this way: "Is God willing to prevent evil, but not able? Then he is not omnipotent. Is he able, but not willing? Then he is malevolent. Is he both able and willing? Then whence cometh evil?"[1]

Now, one way to critique the logical problem of evil is to say that evil is an illusion. But this way out of the problem contradicts common sense, for if anything is hard to deny, it is pain and suffering. Moreover, a consistent Christian cannot deny evil, because the Christian faith recognizes both moral evil, such as vices and sins, and nonmoral evil, such as illness and death.

But a denial of evil is not needed to call into question the logical problem of evil. As Eleonore Stump points out, “The propositions (1) there is suffering in the world and (2) there is an omniscient, omnipotent, perfectly good God are not by themselves logically incompatible.”[2] To hold that God exists and that there is suffering is *not* like holding that the same man is both married and a bachelor. To be a bachelor is to be an unmarried man of marriageable age. If you are married, you cannot at the same time in the same respect also *not* be married. A married bachelor is a self-contradictory notion, like a square circle. Jeremy Bentham provides other self-contradictory concepts: “a species of cold heat, a sort of dry moisture, a kind of resplendent darkness.”[3] It would indeed be a logical contradiction to say, “There is suffering in the world,” and also say, “There is no suffering in the world.” It would be a logical contradiction to assert, “There is an omniscient, omnipotent, perfectly good God,” and also to assert, “There is *not* an omniscient, omnipotent, perfectly good God.” But there is no inherent contraction in holding that (1) there is suffering in the world and that (2) there is an omniscient, omnipotent, perfectly good God.

The logical version of the problem of evil assumes that a good agent must *always* prevent *all* the suffering that he has the power to prevent. But this is not true. A good coach could prevent the suffering of the members of the team by having them avoid vigorous training. Yet even though the coach knows with certainty that practice will be arduous, the coach has a good reason for subjecting athletes to hard training. An experienced dentist can foresee that a root canal will cause some suffering for the patient, but they both judge rightly that the suffering brought about by the root canal is justified. Good parents bring children into the world knowing with 100 percent certainty that someday their children will die. But parents judge rightly that having children is good for them as a couple and good for the children themselves. A good agent does not *always* prevent *all* the suffering that he or she has the power to prevent. Thus, a good God may permit evil, including the evil that we choose, for a good purpose.

So, the logical problem of evil, though popular in the mid-twentieth century, has been widely recognized by contemporary philosophers as a failure to disprove the existence of God. A hangover is no reason to think that God does not exist. But a hangover may make you feel like the man described by Cormac McCarthy: "His head was pounding and his vision skewed in some way and he was vaguely amazed at being alive and not sure that it was worth it."[4]

24

Does Pointless Evil Disprove God's Existence?

The Evidential Problem of Evil

As we saw in the last chapter, the existence of evil is not inherently incompatible with an omnipotent and omnibenevolent being. God may have good reasons to allow some evils to exist. But the second version of the problem of evil—the evidential version—argues that the existence of unnecessary evils disproves God's existence. It can be formulated in two premises: (1) If there are pointless (or gratuitous) evils in the world, then God does not exist. (2) There are pointless evils in the world. Therefore, God does not exist. What is meant here by "pointless" or "gratuitous" evil? Pointless evils are evils that are not justified by some higher good or by avoiding some greater evil.

How do we know that there are pointless evils? We might answer that question by considering its opposite. How do we know when a particular evil is *not* pointless?

It is not pointless for a man to die in successfully defending his family from an attacker intent on murdering them all. It is better for the man to die and save his family than for the man and his entire family to die. It is not pointless for the kidnapper who has committed a crime to suffer the loss of freedom in prison. If kidnappers were not punished, people who were tempted to kidnap might not be deterred from kidnapping. So, a just punishment, though evil for the one who gets punished, is justified as a deterrent to potential wrongdoers. Moreover, if kidnappers were not caught and punished, they could continue their kidnapping, endangering and terrifying more people in the community. So, defense of the community is another justification for punishment. And, in some cases, getting caught and convicted actually helps the wrongdoer. Some people will only stop doing evil if someone else prevents them from doing it. They will only begin to reform when punished for their wrongdoing. Moreover, there is good intrinsically in a just punishment. A just punishment deprives the wrongdoer of a good that the wrongdoer is no longer worthy of enjoying. So, it is good that the robber has to return stolen goods, even though this may cause suffering for the robber.

How do we know that a particular evil has a point, rather than being pointless? Sometimes we can see the point ourselves. We often choose to bring about suffering because we can see that it will secure a greater good or help us avoid a greater evil. It is worth the suffering of going to the dentist to have cavities filled and infections prevented.

Yet, it is undoubtedly true that we can go through suffering and *not* see the point of the suffering. But if I cannot see the point of my suffering, it hardly follows that there is no point to my suffering. After all, I've often experienced what seemed like pointless suffering at the time, only to realize later that good, indeed great good, came out of this suffering. Almost everyone can think back on times in their lives when something bad happened that led to something good. The story of the Chinese farmer from chapter 22 illustrates that unforeseen good can come out of suffering.

Here's another way to express the idea. Let's say that you cannot see the point of $E = mc^2$. Someone then tries to clarify it for you: "The energy (E) of a particle in its rest frame is the product of its mass (m) with the speed of light squared (c^2)." Even with this clarification, you might still not see the meaning or purpose of this scientific formula. Does it follow that there is no meaning or purpose if you or I cannot understand the formula right now? Perhaps we could come to understand if we took a university physics course, but for now we cannot. That hardly shows that there is no meaning or purpose to the formula in question.

So too, from the fact that someone does not see the point of a particular episode of suffering, it hardly follows that there is no point to suffering. Human understanding is limited. There are countless things that we collectively do not know—for example, how to cure all forms of cancer—but it hardly follows that there is no cure for cancer or that we will never know the cure for cancer. Our current ignorance is no reason to believe that an answer is impossible. Humility acknowledges both the limitations of our current knowledge and the possibility of greater knowledge.

As Justin P. McBrayer points out:

> Skeptical theism is the view that God exists but that we should be skeptical of our ability to discern God's reasons for acting or refraining from acting in any particular instance. In particular, says the skeptical theist, we should not grant that *our* inability to think of a good reason for doing or allowing something is indicative of whether or not *God* might have a good reason for doing or allowing something. If there is a God, he knows much more than we do about the relevant facts, and thus it would not be surprising at all if he has reasons for doing or allowing something that we cannot fathom.[1]

Just because we may not know right now why God allows a particular evil, it does not follow that the evil in question is pointless. It is a fallacy to reason, "I don't know why X happened," and then conclude, "Therefore X is pointless."

As Elisabeth Elliot said, "God is God. If He is God, He is worthy of my worship and my service. I will find rest nowhere but in His will, and that will is infinitely, immeasurably, unspeakably beyond my largest notions of what He is up to."[2] Or, as Timothy Keller put it, "Just because you can't see or imagine a good reason why God might allow something to happen doesn't mean there can't be one."[3]

25

Why Is There Evil?

Eleonore Stump on Faith and the Defeat of Suffering

In the last two chapters, we saw that the existence of evil does not disprove the existence of God, and that he may very well have good reasons for allowing evil. But what could those reasons be? The personal experience of suffering—as well as the sheer amount present in the world—often makes it difficult to imagine that any reason could justify its existence. "Each new morn, new widows howl, new orphans cry, new sorrows strike heaven on the face," as Shakespeare wrote in *Macbeth*.[1] Suffering is still the strongest objection to God's existence. One of the best replies to this objection is Eleonore Stump's magisterial *Wandering in Darkness: Narrative and the Problem of Suffering*. In the short span of this chapter, I cannot adequately summarize Stump's argument, let alone adequately deal with the problem of pain. But I hope to provide some sense of Stump's insights so as to encourage more people to delve into this masterwork on the strongest objection to God's existence.

Stump aims to provide a defense of the view that God's existence is not incompatible with the reality of suffering, and that it is possible that God is justified in allowing suffering. Just as a person accused of a crime is innocent until proven guilty beyond a reasonable doubt, so too it is reasonable to believe in God—given the philosophical reasons outlined earlier in this book—until it is proven beyond a reasonable doubt that suffering disproves his existence.

And what exactly is suffering? Stump distinguishes two kinds. One kind of suffering is a lack of objective human flourishing. We suffer when we lack health (sickness), friends (loneliness), or knowledge (ignorance). The other kind of suffering arises when the desires of our hearts are thwarted. These deep desires are subjective and relative to each of us as individuals. For one person, it might be the desire to win the metro league championship in soccer; for another person, it might be the desire to have a relationship with a particular person or to have a child. We can suffer when our flourishing is diminished (say, by getting cancer), and we can also suffer when the desires of our hearts are thwarted (say, by losing a relationship we greatly desire). Stump writes, "What is bad about the evil a human being suffers is that it undermines (partly or entirely) her flourishing, or it deprives her (in part or in whole) of the desires of her heart, or both."[2]

We can, however, be mistaken about either our flourishing or the desires of our heart. If I am a hypochondriac, I may be convinced that I have cancer while I am actually healthy. I might think that I will never attain my heart's desire, but in reality, fulfillment of this desire might be right around the corner. Stump remarks, "If what is bad about suffering is that it undermines a person's flourishing or that it deprives her of the desires of her heart or both, then a benefit that constitutes a morally sufficient reason for God's allowing suffering must be something that somehow defeats the badness of suffering so understood."[3] To defeat suffering is to receive something in exchange that justifies the allowance of that suffering.

Stump explores what could defeat suffering using the philosophical reflection of analytic rigor. However, she notes, "Precise, compelling arguments are not everything. If we insist on rigor above everything else, we are in danger of getting it above everything else: a fossilized view of the world, unable to account for the richness of the reality in which we live our lives."[4]

So supplementing her rigorous philosophical "Dominican" approach is a "Franciscan" narrative approach to knowledge.

Franciscan knowledge cannot be had from deductive arguments alone but is a knowledge of personal experience, stories, and first-person perspective. A great scholar of Abraham Lincoln today has Dominican knowledge of the sixteenth president, but Lincoln's friends and children had Franciscan knowledge of him. Stump points out that a person who visits China regularly cannot, in Dominican knowledge, transmit all she knows as Franciscan knowledge about China. So too, any transformative experience cannot be put entirely into words that adequately capture what takes place in the experience. We cannot adequately explain what seeing the color blue is like to a person born blind.

One of the best ways to gain Franciscan knowledge is through stories. In order to help us grow in Franciscan knowledge, Stump uses narratives from history (such as the life of the poet John Milton) as well as the concrete details of suffering found in the biblical stories of Job, Samson, Abraham, and Mary of Bethany. Each of these individuals suffers in a distinctive way, and Stump explicates their stories with exquisite attention to detail. The story of Job is the story of the suffering of the innocent. By contrast, Samson is his own worst enemy and brings grievous suffering upon himself. Abraham suffers because his heart's desire, to become the father of a great family, is repeatedly thwarted. Finally, Mary of Bethany's suffering consists of heartbrokenness and shame that arise from feeling rejected by Jesus.

In her detailed and nuanced readings of these stories, Stump shows how God allows the suffering of Job, Samson, Abraham, and Mary to bring good to them as individuals, to fulfill the desires of their hearts, and to help them achieve deeper human flourishing than they would have had without the suffering. Following Aquinas, Stump argues that God only allows my suffering for my own sake, much as a parent allows the suffering of a child receiving chemotherapy treatments in order to help the child overcome cancer. Since each person is unique, the suffering of each person is geared toward helping that individual person. As Fr. Paul Mankowski noted:

> I have never yet met anyone who thought that God gave him the right cross to bear (including myself); everyone looks around with a certain wistful envy at others and says to himself, "Now THAT is the kind of cross I could carry with equanimity, courage, even joy." But of course what makes a cross a cross is that it kills the one who carries it; it puts to death that part of the disciple that God knows must die for salvation to work.[5]

God can be likened to an expert surgeon who tailors the scalpel to cut only what needs to be cut from this individual patient.

Abraham, for example, deeply desired to become the father of a large family and suffered because of the sterility of his marriage. But he endured through the suffering and, in the end, did get the desire of his heart. Even to this day, the children of Abraham, the Jewish people, continue to exist. Their ancient enemies—the Hittites, Amorites, Canaanites, Perizzites, Hittites, and Jebusites—are all gone. The agnostic French King Louis XIV once demanded that his counselor Blaise Pascal prove to him that God existed in an argument using only two words. The counselor replied, "The Jews!" Yet not only Jews but also Christians and Muslims consider Abraham their father in faith. It was precisely through his suffering that Abraham became the father in faith to more than half of the human beings now on planet Earth.

Every human being is the hero of his or her own story, but each person's story is also part of a larger story with various other characters. Like a master storyteller, God cares about each of his characters and providentially arranges and interweaves each life journey using suffering to bring about good.

But suffering is still suffering, and no one enjoys it. Stump does not deny the toll that suffering can take on individuals. The fact that God can bring good out of evil does not change evil into good. Mothers Against Drunk Driving has done immeasurable good, but the deaths of children in drunk-driving accidents is always an evil. Evil remains evil, and good remains good, even though evil can arise from good and good can arise from evil.

Stump writes, “On Aquinas’s theodicy, God is justified in allowing human beings to endure suffering such as that experienced by Job, Samson, Abraham, and Mary in the stories, because, through their suffering and only by its means, God gives to each of the protagonists something that these sufferers are willing to trade their suffering to receive, once they understand the nature of what they are being given.”[6] In other words, the ones who suffer can come to recognize, either in this life or in the life to come, that the suffering they endured was justified given the good they received from God through it. Suffering can be defeated.

Stump continues:

> The benefit defeating a person’s suffering has to do either with enabling a person to have the best thing for human beings or with enabling him to ward off the worst thing for human beings; and, in the process, it also offers the sufferer the desires of his heart, compatible with his flourishing. The benefit is, therefore, a matter of offering the sufferer what that sufferer cares about, either as regards flourishing, or as regards the desires of the heart when those desires are interwoven with the flourishing of the sufferer, or both. Plainly, then, the benefit outweighs the suffering.[7]

For Stump, the desires of the heart and the highest human flourishing converge in God. What every heart desires is the fullness of truth, a goodness without evil, and a flawless beauty that is found in God alone. Our highest human flourishing in our minds, in our wills, and in our hearts finds culmination in God. Unfortunately, we can choose to turn away from love of God and neighbor into self-willed loneliness.

As we saw earlier, God cannot do what is not possible. Even God cannot force a human being to freely love him in return. If God wills that each human person be free, then God would contradict his own will if he also willed that the human person not be free. God does not contradict himself. But God’s love never tires in seeking after a loving relationship with each human person. The

Venerable Fulton Sheen once said, “Sometimes the only way the good Lord can get into some hearts is to break them.”[8] The Divine Physician can use suffering as a bitter medicine to heal someone of self-willed loneliness.

For Stump, the problem of suffering must be seen in the wider context of salvation. If all we had were this world, then the suffering that exists would not be justified. On the other hand, if Jesus is right that this life on earth is not our only life, the possibility of eternal salvation is necessary for thinking adequately about suffering. As Fr. Walter J. Ciszek said, “The greatest grace God can give [someone] is to send him a trial he cannot bear with his own powers—and then sustain him with his grace so he may endure to the end and be saved.”[9] Ciszek knew something about suffering after spending twenty-three years in hard labor in the Gulag in Siberia and in Moscow’s infamous Lubyanka prison.

The problem of pain is an allegation of inconsistency in Christian belief, but this alleged inconsistency cannot simply ignore other aspects of Christian belief that Stump believes unravel it. Suppose someone were to allege that two articles of the US Constitution are inconsistent with each other. If other articles of the Constitution resolve the alleged inconsistency, there would in fact be no contradiction in the Constitution, even if it seemed as if there were a contradiction.

So too, Stump’s *Wandering in Darkness* puts the problem of pain back into the overall context of Christian belief. She uses biblical stories, contemporary psychology, and the best of recent philosophy to reconsider the most ancient of problems. The problem of pain is the greatest obstacle to belief in God. To my mind, Stump gives the very best treatment of this crucial issue. But is her appeal to stories, especially biblical stories, problematic? Is the Bible a book worth reading or merely a useless relic of ignorant nomads wandering in the desert? To a short consideration of the problems raised to belief in the Bible we now turn.

Believing in the God of the Bible

26

Does Jesus Reveal God?

The Blind Men and the Elephant, the Rajah and the Christ

The story of the blind men and the elephant is found in ancient Jain, Hindu, and Buddhist philosophers dating all the way back to 500 BC. The parable is meant to illustrate human fallibility in light of the divine mystery.

> The first blind man put out his hand and touched the side of the elephant. "How smooth! An elephant is like a wall." The second blind man put out his hand and touched the trunk of the elephant. "How round! An elephant is like a snake." The third blind man put out his hand and touched the tusk of the elephant. "How sharp! An elephant is like a spear." The fourth blind man put out his hand and touched the leg of the elephant. "How tall! An elephant is like a tree." The fifth blind man reached out his hand and touched the ear of the elephant. "How wide! An elephant is like a fan." The sixth blind man put out his hand and touched the tail of the elephant. "How thin! An elephant is like a rope."
>
> An argument ensued, each blind man thinking his own perception of the elephant was the correct one. The Rajah, awakened by the commotion, called out from the balcony. "The elephant is a big animal," he said. "Each man touched only one part. You must put all the parts together to find out what an elephant is like."

> Enlightened by the Rajah's wisdom, the blind men reached agreement. "Each one of us knows only a part. To find out the whole truth we must put all the parts together."

So, too—according to one interpretation of this story—the various perspectives people offer about ultimate questions are just so many partial experiences that only capture a part of the divine mystery. Human beings seeking to understand the transcendent are like blind men. No one has the full truth; every perspective is partial. Only the Rajah, whose father rules the kingdom, sees the whole elephant and enlightens those who accept his perspective.

What would Thomas Aquinas say about the story of the blind men and the elephant? He would agree that no one has the *full* truth about God except God alone. Only a divine mind can fully comprehend the divine essence, for only an infinite, divine understanding can be comprehensively united with an infinite, divine reality. Even for those in heaven, God remains utterly transcendent, beyond comprehensive human understanding, for those in heaven still have finite minds. For those on earth, the transcendent is even more mysterious. As St. Paul wrote, "For now we see through a glass, darkly; but then face to face: now I know in part; but then shall I know even as also I am known" (1 Cor 13:12, KJV). Human beings cannot fully know the mystery of God. "If I knew him, I would be him," as a medieval Hebrew saying put it.

But what about the Rajah? He has sight, so he knows the truth about the elephant. His vision of the elephant transcends the partial, fragmentary understanding of the blind men who can only touch parts of the elephant. So, at least the Rajah knows the truth about the divine mystery.

But this is a problem for the parable of the blind men and the elephant. As Timothy Keller notes, "The only way you could possibly know that every religion only sees *part* of the truth is if you assume that *you* see all the truth."[1] So, at its heart, the elephant analogy is self-defeating. In his book *The Reason for God: Belief in an Age of Skepticism*, Keller sums up the contradiction inherent in the ancient story: "How could you know that each blind man only sees part of the elephant unless you claim to be able to see the whole elephant?"[2] In other words, "How could you possibly know that no religion can see the whole truth unless you yourself have the superior, comprehensive knowledge of spiritual reality you just claimed that none of the religions have?"[3]

Indeed, if the Rajah is merely human, how can the Rajah transcend the limitations of human experience? He cannot. No one who is merely human can go beyond the *limitations* of being human. If the Rajah is merely human, then he must share in the partial and limited human perspective, and thus he would be just one more blind man.

But what if the divine reality became a human reality? What if God was one of us? Well, if this happened, this human being could know more about God than would ever be possible for a mere human being. This human being could transcend the limitations of human reasoning and finite experience, since this human being would be not only human but also divine.

That is, of course, precisely what Jesus of Nazareth claimed. He said, "I am the way, and the truth, and the life" (Jn 14:6). He said, "I and [God] the Father are one" (Jn 10:30). He said, "He who has seen me has seen the Father" (Jn 14:9). Jesus, the Prince of Peace, claimed the insight of the Rajah in the parable by saying, "I am the light of the world; he who follows me will not walk in darkness, but will have the light of life" (Jn 8:12). If Jesus is God from God, then Jesus can accurately tell us about the divine mystery. To find out the whole truth of the divine mystery, God must put all the parts together for us. Indeed, if Jesus is God, he can give sight to blind men (Mt 20:29–34). Thus, the parable of the blind men and the elephant leads either to contradiction or to Christ.

In the next chapter, we will examine whether the claims of Jesus—such as that "he who has seen me has seen the Father" and that God is Father, Son, and Holy Spirit—are contrary to reason.

27

Does Aquinas Contradict Himself?

On the Mysteries of Faith

Aquinas thought that some truths that God reveals to us can be known as true through reason. As we've seen in this book, we can know through reason that there's just one God, that God is intelligent, that God has a will, and that God is love. We can learn these "preambles of faith" through philosophy, through arguments that are based *not* on revelation but on principles that are available to all people of goodwill.

There are also, Aquinas argues, "mysteries of faith," such as the truth that Jesus is God. Thomas thinks that is something that we cannot know through philosophy. Rather, we know Jesus is God through revelation. We come to believe that Jesus is God because we trust what Jesus says. Similarly, the idea that God is three Persons—Father, Son, and Holy Spirit—is not, in Aquinas's view, something that reason alone can show to be true. Are these claims contrary to reason?

Well, Aquinas's view would be that, no, they're not. They go *beyond* reason. Reason can't show that they're true. But they're not *against* reason. In a similar way, imagine if a friend of yours says, "My parents were the most amazing people in the world. Too bad you never got to meet them." What your friend says doesn't go against reason, but it does go beyond what you know on the basis of your own experience.

But let's say everything you know about this friend is compatible with the idea that this friend of yours had great parents. Your friend is honest and trustworthy. You might have faith and believe that what your friend said to you is true.

Aquinas says a similar thing about the mysteries of faith. Yes, they go beyond reason, but they're not contrary to reason. God is perfectly trustworthy. God can neither deceive nor be deceived because he is the source of all truth and is the truth himself. Statements like these naturally raise an important philosophical question, a question also made famous when Jesus was asked by Pontius Pilate, "What is truth?"

The gospels record no word from Jesus in reply to this question. But Aristotle defined truth as the correspondence of mind and reality. Working with this understanding of truth, Aquinas came to the conclusion that God is the purest truth. God's mind and God's reality are the very same thing, for (as we talked about in a previous chapter) God is not composed of any parts, so God cannot be composed of his essence plus his intelligence. As human beings, we exist first as babies before we are intelligent. If we become cognitively disabled, we continue to be human beings, but we may no longer be intelligent. So, what we are in essence (human beings) is not the same as what we do (understand things). There is, in God, a perfect unity in the divine intelligence and the divine essence, for they are the very same thing.

Indeed, God is the First Truth because God is the First Cause. The truth is in our minds when what we think corresponds to reality. If I think the cat is on the mat, and the cat really is on the mat, then my mind knows the truth about where the cat is. This everyday truth presupposes the First Truth, for without God as the First Cause, there would be no mat, no cat, and no mind for me to know it.

Since God is the First Truth, which grounds every other truth about cats, mats, and us, God cannot be mistaken about anything.

God's knowledge is perfect because God knows himself perfectly as the First Cause. As an artist with self-knowledge knows what art he or she has made, so too God knows everything that he causes. As noted earlier, God is also perfectly good, rather than (as we are) a combination of good and evil, virtue and vice, uprightness and corruption. Finally, Thomas Aquinas holds along with both his Catholic predecessors, like Augustine, and successors, such as the *Catechism of the Catholic Church*, that lying is always wrong. "A *lie* consists in speaking a falsehood with the intention of deceiving. The Lord denounces *lying* as the work of the devil" (*CCC*, 2482).

Now if we put these thoughts together, it follows that whatever God reveals is maximally trustworthy. Merely human teachers are not maximally trustworthy because they can be mistaken and communicate to you in good faith (but mistakenly) what they think is true. But God cannot be intellectually mistaken. If God is the First Truth, if God is purest Truth, God's knowledge of himself and everything else must be infallible and perfect. Likewise, a human teacher might lie to you. But if God is perfectly good, then God does not do evil acts such as lying. So, if God communicates anything to us, that communication is maximally trustworthy and worthy of belief. Catholics believe that the fullness of revelation is a Person, Jesus of Nazareth. What he says and what he does reveals to us who God is.

But here's a problem. If Aquinas is right that Jesus is God, and if he's right that human knowledge is not like divine knowledge, then does Jesus know like God or does Jesus know like a human being? And if Aquinas is right that Jesus is God, then is Aquinas wrong that God does not have a body? Again, there seems to be a contradiction in Aquinas's view; it seems that Aquinas goes against reason. If Aquinas is right that Jesus is God, then is Aquinas wrong that an eternal God has no potency to suffer and die? Here again, we see a potential contradiction in Aquinas. And so faith and reason would seem to be opposed rather than in harmony.

How does St. Thomas answer these difficulties? Drawing on the teaching of the church fathers and the decrees of church councils, Aquinas holds that Jesus has two natures, a divine nature and a human nature. This distinction between divine nature and human nature helps Thomas to overcome these difficulties. Let me explain how this works.

First, we have to distinguish between a nature and a person. The question, "*What* is it?" is the question that is answered by a thing's nature. So, if you say, "What is that thing over there?" Well, it's a tree, or it's a dog, or it's a human being. The nature of a thing is what the thing is—for example, a human being *is* a rational animal, a living, sensing thing capable of abstract thought—and nature determines what an individual can do. So if an individual is a tree, it can do certain things like photosynthesis. If an individual is a dog, the dog can bark and wag its tail and hear at a frequency outside of what humans can hear. And if you're a human being, well, that nature gives you the ability to do things like make jokes and compose poetry.

Now, the question, "*Who* is it?" is the question that corresponds to what a *person* is. The person is the individual who does the activity in question. Who does the reasoning? Who writes the poetry? The person is the individual who knowingly and freely does these activities.

In some cases, like an oak tree, there is one nature, but no person. An oak tree has a nature, it can do certain things, but it's not a person because it is not an individual who freely does any of those things. An oak tree doesn't decide, "I'm going to do photosynthesis today," or "I'm going to drop some acorns today." It automatically, in virtue of its nature, does whatever it does. So, there can be one nature but no person. Let's now consider a different example.

Sheila is a person, and she has a human nature. Because she has a human nature, she can do certain things. She can write short stories, she can sew costumes, and she can talk to her kids. And she also is a person, so she's an individual who knowingly and willingly can do those things. Unlike the oak tree, which automatically does photosynthesis, Sheila, as a person, can exercise the various operations that her nature allows her to exercise, like writing poetry and sewing costumes. In the case of Sheila, you have one nature and one person.

Now, in the case of Jesus, you have two natures and one person. In his divine nature, Jesus is eternal, without a beginning and without an end. In his divine nature, Jesus has no body, for reasons we've talked about earlier. In his divine nature, Jesus cannot suffer or die. In his divine nature, Jesus has divine knowledge and a divine will. So Jesus, in Aquinas's view, is fully divine.

But Christ is also fully human, and so he has a full human nature. The human nature of Jesus is not eternal, but comes into existence in the womb of his mother, Mary. Jesus, in his human nature, does have a body. Jesus, in his human nature, can suffer and can die. Jesus, in his human nature, has human knowledge. So, Jesus in his human nature, knew things through his senses. He would see things and hear things. He would remember things, and he could, in his human nature, grow in wisdom. Jesus, also in his human nature, has a human will.

So the bottom line is this. There is no contradiction whatsoever in Thomas holding both that God has no body, and that Jesus is God and has a body. It is perfectly consistent to hold *both* that God is eternal, and that Jesus in his human nature is not eternal but in his divine nature is eternal. There is nothing unreasonable about holding this belief. Indeed, since God is trustworthy, it is entirely reasonable to believe whatever God reveals, including the divinity of Jesus.

This brings us to another important topic, the relationship of God with God. If there's only one God, what does God think about? If God is an intelligent being, he must think about something. And if there's only one God, who does God love? For to be happy, one must love. Does the First Cause turn out to be an egoist God, sitting in solitary splendor, and reduced to loving himself as a selfish deity? Well, Aquinas would answer that question with a no.

God thinks and knows himself. You might say God is an eternal thinker who thinks an eternal thought, which you could call an eternal Word. That thought or Word is infinite and equal to himself, a Person who is unique and absolute. The eternal thinker and the eternal thought share an eternal love.

Thomas is talking about the Holy Trinity. You have the eternal thinker, the Father; who has an eternal thought, the Son; and they share an eternal love, the Holy Spirit. These are three Persons in one God. They share one nature as God, yet they are three different Persons: the Father, and the Son, and the Holy Spirit.

You might say they are like a heavenly family into which we are offered adoption. To be offered adoption is a great gift. It is to be welcomed into a family, even though you're not, biologically speaking, a member of that family. Once you're adopted, you become a true member of that family.

God, in Aquinas's view, invites us to be part of that heavenly family, to be an adopted child of God. And to become an adopted child of God is to begin to share in God's own perfect happiness. God, in himself, is perfectly happy. God's intellect is perfectly satisfied with God's truth, and God's will is perfectly satisfied with God's goodness. In God, nothing whatsoever is missing.

When we come into a relationship with God, we begin to share some part of this divine happiness. We have an intellect, and our intellect is satisfied by the truth. God is that perfect truth. Our will seeks what's good, and God is that perfect goodness. God is also perfect love because the Divine Persons love each other perfectly. When we connect with God, we have some share in God's perfect goodness. The Trinity, in other words, is connected very deeply to our own happiness. Heaven is where we find, in the fullness of God, those things that slake the thirst of hearts, satisfy the hunger of starving minds, and give rest to unrequited love.

Heaven is, you might say, the communion with perfect life, perfect truth, and perfect love. If we're going to have this perfect happiness, we need to have a perfected relationship with Perfect Happiness. The biblical stories portray how the God of Perfect Happiness has worked in the lives of people both before and after Jesus.

28

Is the Bible Meaningful?

Jordan Peterson on Archetypal Readings of Scripture

In his book *We Who Wrestle with God: Perceptions of the Divine*, Jordan Peterson addresses the biblical stories that shape narratives of our culture from *Hamlet* to *Wicked*, from Dostoevsky's *Brothers Karamazov* to Disney's *Lion King*. He focuses particular attention on the stories of Adam and Eve, Cain and Abel, Noah, the Tower of Babel, Abraham, Moses, and Jonah. I've explored Peterson's earlier interpretations of these stories elsewhere in my book *Jordan Peterson, God, and Christianity.*

To interpret these stories, Peterson draws on his expertise in clinical psychology, as well as on evolutionary biology, political history, and insights from Milton, Nietzsche, Jung, Popper, Solzhenitsyn, and J. K. Rowling. In comparison to his earlier YouTube lectures on the Bible, *We Who Wrestle with God* shows considerable development in depth and breadth, in part by utilizing insights gleaned from his online seminars on Exodus.

Peterson begins by noting that a vast number of objects present themselves to our senses and that there are likewise a vast number of ways to focus our perceptions of these objects. So, how do we prioritize our perceptions?

What we value enables us to turn the chaos of sense perception into the order of human action. As Peterson puts it, "We perceive, therefore, in accordance with our aim."[1] If I give you $1,000 for each blue thing you notice in your vicinity, you'll start to notice blue things that you didn't notice before. If the reward were for finding living things, you'd focus on living things instead of blue things.

Aims shape our perceptions, and narratives shape our aims. The stories we are told and the stories we tell ourselves shape what we seek. Here, Peterson echoes the insight of Alasdair MacIntyre, who wrote in *After Virtue*: "Man is in his actions and practice, as well as in his fictions, essentially a story-telling animal. . . . I can only answer the question 'What am I to do' if I can answer the prior question 'Of what story or stories do I find myself a part?'"[2] Stories also shape our desires. As René Girard notes, "We desire what others desire because we imitate their desires."[3] Stories teach us what others desire, thereby shaping our own desires.

Given this framework, *We Who Wrestle with God* is not reserved for those who view the Bible as divinely inspired or those who "believe in God"—a phrase Peterson problematizes in a way similar to Thomas Aquinas, who distinguishes three senses of believing in God. In Peterson's view, every one of us is fated to wrestle with God, though perhaps not as Jacob did in the biblical story (Gn 32:22–32). "God" is, in one of Peterson's characterizations, whatever our final end is—that to which other things are ultimately ordered and sacrificed. If we are to move forward, we need a goal. Proximate goals arise because of more remote goals, and the ultimate goal functions for us as "God." In this analysis, Peterson echoes Aristotle's understanding of human action in the *Nicomachean Ethics* as well as Paul Tillich's idea that our "God" is whatever functions as the object of our ultimate concern. As Peterson puts it, "When attention must be prioritized and action undertaken, no atheism is possible. Something must be elevated and all other things sacrificed."[4]

Peterson sees the biblical stories as portraying God as various "characters." God is a creative spirit walking with Adam. God is the summons to prepare given to Noah. God is the call to adventure for Abraham. God is the dreadful spirit of freedom for Moses.

And God is a voice of truth urging Jonah to break his lying silence for the good of his enemies. These stories reveal different aspects of God's nature.

With due respect to his critics, Peterson is not aiming to provide a historical-critical interpretation of scripture in the literal sense. His attention to context, ancient languages, and multiple translations shows he is also not by any means ignoring the specificity of the biblical text. But he isn't writing for scholars interested in Akkadian loanwords in biblical Hebrew. He is writing for those who want to think deeply about the stories that shape our culture. Judging Peterson's archetypal reading of biblical stories as a poor historical-critical interpretation is like judging Michael Jackson's *Thriller* as a bad sculpture.

Peterson's critics are also mistaken when they construe him as an advocate of a kind of radical individualism. On the contrary, Peterson emphasizes, "*We inevitably exist, as human beings, in relationship*"[5] (italics in the original). For him, to champion individual rights, including freedom of speech, is not to advocate the expressive individualism of an atomized and buffered self. But avoiding the Scylla of expressive individualism doesn't push Peterson toward the Charybdis of utopian socialism. Here, too, the biblical stories illuminate. Peterson unfolds his account of the dangers of socialist utopias in relation to the story of the Tower of Babel. He notes: "The narrative is not political—or if it is, it is so only in service of a higher or deeper meaning. The same can be said of many of the biblical narratives that mention specific societies or even specific people: they are to be regarded as types or patterns, with what is specific and identifiable used only to characterize a deeper truth."[6] This seeking of the deeper and more universal insight of scripture is found throughout Peterson's book. The stories in scripture are not just about the particular people involved but also about the ever-recurring challenges of the human experience.

Many of the crucial challenges depicted in the Bible concern voluntary agreement either between individuals or—most importantly—between individuals and God. God makes such agreements, known as "covenants," with Adam, Noah, Abraham, Moses, and David. Jesus establishes a new covenant. According to Peterson, *contract* and *covenant* are synonymous. He writes, "What precisely is a covenant? A contract between two parties who agree to undertake or refrain from undertaking certain acts: a contract, compact, deal or bargain."[7] However, prolific author and scripture scholar Scott Hahn draws a sharp contrast between *covenant* and *contract* in the Bible. In *A Father Who Keeps His Promises*, Hahn writes:

> A contract is the exchange of property in the form of goods and services ("That is mine and this is yours"); whereas a covenant calls for the exchange of persons ("I am yours and you are mine"), creating a shared bond of interpersonal communion. For ancient Israelites, a covenant differed from a contract about as much as marriage differed from prostitution. When a man and woman marry, they declare before God their undying love to one another until death, but a prostitute sells her body to the highest bidder and then moves on to the next customer. So contracts make people customers, employees, clients; whereas covenants turn them into spouses, parents, children, siblings. In short, covenants are made to forge bonds of sacred kinship.[8]

This distinction between covenant and contract can shape how scripture as a whole is to be understood. Hahn notes, "If you want to get to the heart of Scripture, think covenant not contract, father not judge, family room not courtroom."[9]

In any case, Peterson's psychological analysis reveals the significant ways the Bible has shaped our culture. For instance, he notes the many ways the biblical stories address family dynamics, such as the covenant of marriage. He writes, "Long-term monogamous strategies are therefore not only the human norm, cross culturally speaking, but also the correct ideal."[10] Peterson is right that there are abundant empirical grounds for preferring monogamy to polygamy. Monogamy is better for women, who are more likely to experience equality in marriage; better for children, who are more likely to receive good care; and better for men, who are more likely to have a chance of getting married. Given roughly equal numbers of men and women in most times and places, if one man has one hundred wives, then one hundred men have no wives. So, in a polygamous society, more men will be excluded from finding a wife, since a few men have more than one wife, leaving many men with no wives. The biblical stories themselves portray the discord arising from polygamy, as Peterson notes in the story of Abraham, Sarah, and Hagar. Despite the discord polygamy brings, according to Harvard University Professor of Human Evolutionary Biology Joseph Henrich, "The anthropological record indicates that approximately 85 per cent of human societies have permitted men to have more than one wife."[11] What accounts for the worldwide switch from default polygamy in ancient times to default monogamy today? In *The WEIRDest People in the World: How the West Became Psychologically Peculiar and Particularly Prosperous*, Henrich answers that the Catholic Church's teachings on marriage gave rise to free markets, inalienable rights, and democracy. According to Henrich, it is the biblical stories, as understood in the Catholic tradition, that gave rise to these goods.

The stories of the Bible are among the most influential stories of the human condition, in its frailty and glory, in its fragility and resilience. Peterson is convinced that engagement with the rich and deep stories of the Bible can help us write a better version of the story of our lives. In *We Who Wrestle with God*, Peterson offers archetypal readings of the Bible that are personal, literary, historical, ethical, multidisciplinary, and imaginative to help readers aim higher. If the arguments of earlier chapters of this book are right, the Bible may be even more important than suggested by Peterson. If God does exist, and if God loves us, then it is reasonable to think that God would want a deeper relationship with us. Friends share secrets with each other. So too, the Christian belief is that God reveals himself to human beings. The Bible recounts stories of divine and human interaction. The gospels claim that the Author of the cosmos became a character in the human story. In the next chapters, we will consider some objections to understanding the Bible as revelatory stories of the developing relationship of God and human beings.

29

Is the Bible Deficient?

Sam Harris and Jordan Peterson on Scriptural Credibility

In a viral video released on Christmas Day 2023, Jordan Peterson and the atheist author Sam Harris discussed a wide variety of topics. In contrast to some earlier combative conversations, this discussion explored their differences in a more collaborative way.

Among the most important of the philosophical differences between Peterson and Harris is a fundamental disagreement about the Bible. As described in his book *We Who Wrestle with God*, Peterson sees scripture as containing deep wisdom about the value of sacrifice in making atonement with the highest good. But Harris sees the Bible as an enormous stumbling block:

> I'm effectively an atheist with respect to Christianity, Judaism, and Islam. Despite all of the other things . . . that make me a good candidate for being sympathetic to those traditions, [I reject] the claim about the books [as God's Word]. It's so preposterous, given how easy it would be for an omniscient being to have proven his omniscience in those books. . . . It would be trivially easy for an omniscient being to put a page of text in there that would even now be confounding us with its depths of inspiration, scientifically, ethically in every other sense, right?[1]

Harris is in good company in finding the Bible deficient. In book 3 of his *Confessions*, St. Augustine of Hippo describes a similar negative evaluation of scripture. If the Bible is really the Word of God, Augustine wondered, why is it not written with a greater eloquence than the works of Cicero? Augustine also worried about the problematic ethical elements, especially in the Old Testament. He later learned more sophisticated ways of reading the Bible from St. Ambrose, which changed Augustine's mind.

But neither Augustine nor Ambrose directly addresses the issue raised by Sam Harris. If the Bible really is the Word of God, written by an omniscient Creator, then the Bible should contain scientifically advanced messages that show the intelligence of its divine Author. The book of Genesis could have included the laws of motion articulated by Isaac Newton or the theory of relativity put forward by Albert Einstein. But since the Bible does not reveal such scientific truths but rather shows all the marks of being written by ancient authors utterly ignorant of contemporary science, the Bible must not be the Word of God.

Harris seems to assume that, if God communicates, it would be in a way that overwhelms the human beings who receive the communication. After all, no ancient person possessed sufficient background information to understand Newton's laws or Einstein's theory of relativity, so including such information could only baffle and be unintelligible to the original readers of scripture.

On the other hand, as Cardinal Baronius suggested, maybe the point of scripture is not to teach us scientific knowledge about how the heavens go but spiritual knowledge about how to go to heaven. Indeed, maybe God communicates in a way that does not overwhelm but rather underwhelms. This possibility is expressed in the story of God revealing himself to the prophet Elijah: "The Lord passed by, and a great and strong wind rent the mountains, and broke in pieces the rocks before the Lord, but the Lord was not in the wind; and after the wind an earthquake, but the Lord was not in the earthquake; and after the earthquake a fire, but the Lord was not in the fire; and after the fire a still small voice" (1 Kgs 19:11–12). It is only in the still small voice (conscience?) that

God manifests himself to Elijah. God underwhelms rather than overwhelms him.

Someone taking Harris's view might assume that if God becomes a human being, God would manifest himself as mighty, overwhelming, and powerful. If God became human, he would come down from the clouds as a giant with overpowering strength and weapons to destroy anyone who challenges him. Indeed, the Jews at the time of Jesus looked for a messiah-conqueror who would violently overthrow Roman rule and establish an everlasting Jewish kingdom of this world.

But maybe God enters the world not as a giant with weapons of mass destruction but as an infant swaddled to immobility. According to the Christian story, God arrives not with overpowering strength but in utter vulnerability, weakness, and defenselessness. And when this baby grows to adulthood, he does not lead an army into battle, slaying thousands in his path like Napoleon or Attila the Hun. On the contrary, Jesus freely gives himself over to betrayal, to torture, and then to death. Not force of arms but free acceptance of suffering characterizes the kingdom of Jesus, which he says is not of this world. Not violence but vulnerability is his trademark.

And maybe the Word of God reflects this gentle, humble approach. Unlike the Islamic view in which every word of the Quran is dictated syllable by syllable to Muhammad, the view of Catholic Christians is that the Bible is the divine Word written in human words that reflect their human authors. So what Sam Harris seems to be critiquing is a fundamentalist understanding of scripture, which is itself rejected by the Catholic Church. As Pope Benedict XVI pointed out in his exhortation *Verbum Domini* (*The Word of the Lord*):

> The basic problem with fundamentalist interpretation is that, refusing to take into account the historical character of biblical revelation, it makes itself incapable of accepting the full truth of the incarnation itself. As regards relationships with God, fundamentalism seeks to escape any closeness of the divine

> and the human . . . for this reason, it tends to treat the biblical text as if it had been dictated word for word by the Spirit. It fails to recognize that the word of God has been formulated in language and expression conditioned by various periods. (no. 44)

Harris's critique may legitimately undermine Muslim or Protestant understandings of scripture (they can speak for themselves), but it is a straw-man caricature of the Catholic approach to the Bible. This approach is summarized with brevity and clarity in *Verbum Domini*, sections 36–44. Pope Benedict XVI writes:

> The interpretation of sacred Scripture presupposes, in a word, *the harmony of faith and reason*. On the one hand, it calls for a faith which, by maintaining a proper relationship with right reason, never degenerates into fideism, which in the case of Scripture would end up in fundamentalism. On the other hand, it calls for a reason which, in its investigation of the historical elements present in the Bible, is marked by openness and does not reject *a priori* anything beyond its own terms of reference. In any case, the religion of the incarnate *Logos* can hardly fail to appear profoundly reasonable to anyone who sincerely seeks the truth and the ultimate meaning of his or her own life and history. (no. 36)

This Catholic understanding is more in harmony with Peterson's multivalent method of reading scripture, hence the fundamental disagreement of Peterson and Harris about the Bible.

If this approach is right, God does not communicate via the wind of a hurricane, the ground-shattering force of an earthquake, or the blaze of a roaring fire, but rather through a gentle whisper. God does not become human as a gigantic UFC fighter who lives by the sword but as a swaddled infant and later as a man bound, scourged, and put to death. And, so too, God's Word does not overwhelm with scientific insights utterly unintelligible to the first readers of scripture. Maybe, the ways of God are not the ways of Sam.

30

Is the Bible Dogmatic?

Sam Harris and Jordan Peterson on Fundamental Principles

Whatever "dogma" is, Sam Harris certainly doesn't like it. In the conversation discussed in the previous chapter, Harris repeatedly condemns dogma, and Peterson repeatedly tries to moderate this condemnation. Harris notes correctly that dogma is "a Catholic term."[1] But what exactly is being condemned? The target is moving.

First, Harris defines *dogma* as "a belief that is held in spite of the fact that there's no good evidence for it."[2] According to this definition, belief in God is *not* a dogma. If Aristotle, Augustine, Aquinas, Leibniz, Plantinga, and William Lane Craig are right, there is good evidence to believe that God exists. Indeed, the *Catechism of the Catholic Church* teaches that "by natural reason man can know God with certainty" (50).

But belief in God is not only a dogma but is the fundamental dogma of the Catholic creed. So, Harris's definition of dogma must differ radically from a Catholic understanding of the term. In which case, his critique of dogma is of a straw man of his own invention.

Harris offers a second understanding of dogma: "If I say to you, listen, I believe X and there's nothing you can say to convince me otherwise, and no matter how good your evidence gets, no matter how good your arguments get, I'm not gonna want to hear it. And if you press the case, I'm gonna get angrier and angrier until the possibility of having a conversation about anything fully erodes."[3] *Dogma* in this sense means "close-mindedness."

Yet close-mindedness is a characteristic that can afflict a believer or a skeptic, an atheist or a theist. As woke mobs show us, you can reject all "dogma" in the religious sense of the term and yet be utterly certain of your beliefs and closed off from learning from others. Moreover, you can believe in a dogma (let's say, "God exists") and also not get angry and indeed (as I do) even enjoy talking to people who see things differently. So, "close-mindedness" is a sloppy definition of dogma.

In a third characterization, Harris seems to understand dogma as a belief that leads to harming others. Harris is right that dogma *can* lead to harming others. But anything, even the best of things, can be misused, distorted, degraded. Romantic love can be the beginning of a relationship that lasts a lifetime. But, as countless true-crime episodes indicate, the abuse of romantic love can lead to murder. Likewise, Harris and I share an admiration for the achievements of science. But can science be abused? The answer to this question is found in the scientific experiments conducted at Tuskegee as well as those of Dr. Josef Mengele. So, it hardly counts against dogma that it can lead to bad consequences.

Peterson recognizes this when he says that we should "try to distinguish between religious experience per se, or the religious experience that's valuable and a counterproductive totalitarian dogmatism."[4] Indeed, if someone believes and lives in accordance with the dogma that every single human being deserves respect, this belief would in general help rather than harm people. The world would be a much better place if the dictum attributed to Bernard Lonergan were universally adopted as dogma: "Be attentive, be intelligent, be responsible, be loving, and, if necessary, change."[5]

In a fourth way of using the term, Harris contrasts *dogma* and *method*: "Dogma is not a statement of how good the method was. Dogma is just, we didn't have a method, but this is so. It says so in the book, the book is perfect. How do we know it's perfect? 'Cause the book itself says so, right? That's a dog that bites its own tail. That's not a method. That is dogmatism and in my view, totally illegitimate."[6]

I totally agree with Harris that circular arguments are invalid. But as Karl Keating points out in his book *Catholicism and Fundamentalism*, "[Catholics] are *not* basing the inspiration of the Bible on the Church's infallibility and the Church's infallibility on the word of an inspired Bible. That indeed would be a circular argument."[7] Instead, it is the Church that writes the New Testament, and it is the Church that is the proper interpreter of the New Testament. At least if his target is Catholic belief, Harris has again attacked a straw man.

Harris has confidence in method, and in this too I think he is right. But even the best method cannot be self-authenticating. If I have questions about whether I can trust the empirical method, it hardly helps to gather empirical evidence. If I am unsure whether logically valid deductive arguments show their conclusion, I cannot settle the matter by means of a logically valid deductive argument.

So, as Aristotle noted, first principles are necessary in order to *begin* the process of reasoning. Every method must presuppose some starting points. There is nothing illegitimate or "dogmatic" in a pejorative sense about having first principles in science, in philosophy, or in theology.

As Alvin Plantinga pointed out, "Every train of argument will have to start somewhere, and the ultimate premises from which it starts will not themselves be believed on the evidential basis of other propositions; they will have to be accepted in the *basic* way, that is, not on the evidential basis of other beliefs."[8] Everyone who reasons has basic beliefs, first principles, fundamental axioms, or "dogmas" from which they begin to reason to other conclusions.

There is nothing inherently close-minded, harmful, or viciously circular about intellectual activities arising from first principles or basic beliefs. Mathematicians, philosophers, and scientists all begin to reason from fundamental axioms. Catholics have their own first principles and basic beliefs, like the Nicene Creed.

For Catholics, an accurate definition of *dogma* comes from Cardinal Joseph Ratzinger (later elected Pope Benedict XVI). He wrote that "dogma is by definition nothing other than an interpretation of Scripture."[9] Catholic dogma constitutes the first principles or basic beliefs of Catholics, expressed, for example, in the Nicene Creed. If God actually exists, then it liberates the mind to believe that God exists. If God exists, believing in the dogma of God's existence frees a person to believe and live in accordance with reality. If God does not exist, then it frees the mind to believe in atheism. So, at issue is not so much dogma as what is true.

31

Is the Bible True?

C. S. Lewis and Jordan Peterson on Biblical Stories

Among the most persuasive expositors of Christianity in the twentieth century was C. S. Lewis. Among the most persuasive expositors of the Bible in the twenty-first century is Jordan Peterson. Lewis was a literature professor who explained Christianity to secular audiences. Peterson is a professor emeritus of psychology who today seeks to explain the Bible, especially the stories of Genesis, in ways that resonate with secular audiences.

Both Peterson and Lewis place great value on the power of myth. But what is "myth" exactly? It's an ambiguous term sometimes used to mean an entertaining but false story naive people made up to explain what they did not understand. We could refer to this kind of myth as narrative theoretical ignorance. Myth, in this sense of the term, is of its very nature opposed to facts, science, and truth.

But the term *myth* can also describe a narrative, poetic embodiment of deep insight for human living. We could call this kind of myth narrative practical wisdom. Myth in this sense is not opposed to the facts found by science, but it rather reaches far beyond the empirically verifiable. Myth as narrative practical wisdom embodies what is deeply important to us. As Peterson puts it, "In the mythological world, what matters is what's important. The world is made out of what matters, not of matter. It requires a very different orientation."[1] William Bruce Cameron once made a similar point: "Not everything that can be counted counts, and not everything that counts can be counted."[2] So, insofar as we act, we all necessarily live in the mythological world, a world not reducible simply to the scientific method and what is empirically verifiable.

Atheist intellectuals like Dawkins and Harris argue that only science reveals the truth. But the world as investigated by science does not give us enough information to act in our lives. Science functions something like a metal detector. A metal detector is extremely useful for finding an engagement ring lost in the sand. But a metal detector is not what is needed if a man is deciding whether to give an engagement ring to his girlfriend or for the girlfriend in deciding whether to accept the ring.

Inasmuch as we must act in the world, we embody a view about what is valuable and what is not, and this embodiment follows the pattern of a story. "Everybody acts out a myth," says Peterson, "but very few people know what their myth is. You should know what your myth is, because it might be a tragedy, and maybe you don't want it to be. That's really worth thinking about, because you have a pattern of behavior that characterizes you."[3]

Every culture has its myths, because every culture embodies characteristic patterns of action. Since there is a shared human nature, we would expect these stories to share commonalities. "Because we're all human and because we all share the same biological platform," Peterson explains, "a platform that we share even with animals to a large degree, we tend to interpret the world in very similar ways. Those interpretations are often expressed in stories. The stories are descriptions about how human beings act, and our fundamental problem in the world is how to act."[4]

Nor are these myths confined to the ancient world. "They manifest themselves everywhere. They manifest themselves in movies and in books," notes Peterson. "I mean, Harry Potter is a mythological story. It made Rowling richer than the Queen of England. You know, these stories have power."[5] Stories like the Harry Potter series resonate with readers because they reveal aspects of the world and lessons for how to act that strike the reader as deeply true and necessary, even if they can't be empirically verified. We find these truths in such stories as "Sleeping Beauty" (be courageous in the face of the unknown), "The Lion King" (don't run from responsibility), and "Beauty and the Beast" (love your enemies).

We can find similarities between Christian stories and pagan stories, between narrative practical wisdom as articulated by the children of Abraham and narrative practical wisdom as articulated by the children of Homer. But both Lewis and Peterson agree that the Christian narrative is something special, although for different reasons. According to Peterson, "Christianity has done two things: it's developed the most explicit doctrine of good versus evil, and it's developed the most explicit and articulated doctrine of the logos. And so I would say, in many traditions, it's implicit. It's implicit in hero mythology, for example. I think what happens is that, if you aggregate enough hero myths and extract out the central theme, you end up with the logos. It's the thing that's common to all heroes."[6] For Peterson, the logos is the pattern of being that characterizes the hero, the myth that the heroic person acts out. And if you look at all the heroes in pagan myths and Hebrew writings and extract their greatest characteristics, the greatest of all heroes is Christ. He perfectly embodies every heroic trait. He is loving, courageous, wise, and much more. In Peterson's view, the story of Christ's life is the ultimate myth, the greatest model we have for how to act in the world. Lewis would certainly agree, but he would also have another explanation of the greatness of Christ: the story of Christ is not merely a myth, but the only true myth.

Here, and most importantly, Peterson and Lewis diverge on whether the narrative practical wisdom of the Christian story is also objectively, historically, and theoretically true. Thus far at least, Peterson declines to affirm or deny life after death, claiming that the "mythological landscape," rather than "the objective world," is the landscape of human experience. He primarily sees Christ as a model for how to live this life. Lewis, as a believing

Christian, affirmed life after death in his writings. He saw Jesus Christ as overcoming the greatest threat to man: unlimited pain for an unlimited duration in an unending death, rather than the temporary pain or physical death that man experiences in the flesh. For Lewis, Christ is much more than a mere teacher, saving people from ignorance. Christ is the Savior, saving people for heavenly happiness.

In Lewis's view, "The heart of Christianity is a myth which is also a fact. The old myth of the Dying God, without ceasing to be myth, comes down from the heaven of legend and imagination to the earth of history. It happens—at a particular date, in a particular place, followed by definable historical consequences. We pass from a Balder or an Osiris, dying nobody knows when or where, to a historical Person crucified (it is all in order) under Pontius Pilate. By becoming fact it does not cease to be myth: that is the miracle."[7] Peterson seems, at least so far, to be still considering the question of whether the myth is also a fact. When asked if he has faith, Peterson sometimes replies that he strives to live as if God exists. Fr. Richard John Neuhaus had a striking analysis of such a striving: "If you would believe," he said, "act as though you believe, leaving it to God to know whether you believe, for such leaving it to God is faith."[8] Not bad advice.

Throughout this book, I have examined the relationship of faith and reason. The first part removed errors and obstacles—such as skepticism, scientism, materialism, and pantheism—to clear thinking about God, and by extension clear thinking about Christ. The second part used philosophical arguments to show how certain truths of faith are reasonable. Reason points to the reality of an Uncaused Cause who is one, omniscient, endowed with a will, and loving. However, there are other truths that reason cannot know through its own power, such as that God is Father, Son, and Holy Spirit and that Jesus is true God and true man. Reason can help to remove objections to such beliefs, but it cannot demonstrate that these "mysteries of faith," as Aquinas calls them, are true. To believe that these mysteries of faith revealed by the

Bible are true requires the gift of faith, which is given by God and not by philosophers. We may strive to reach up to God through reason, but God also reaches down to us through revelation. God is a generous giver.

Notes

1. Where to Begin?

1. As quoted by James Wood, "Noble Saves," February 19, 2012, *New Yorker*, https://www.newyorker.com/magazine/2012/02/27/noble-savages.

2. Timothy Keller, "Everyone in the world is an evangelist," X, January 12, 2021, https://x.com/timkellernyc/status/1349074420871135233.

3. Timothy Keller, "Everyone makes exclusive truth claims," X, February 12, 2023, https://x.com/timkellernyc/status/1624823147726794753.

4. Timothy Keller, "To insist doctrine doesn't matter is really a doctrine itself," X, August 13, 2018, https://x.com/timkellernyc/status/1029067309690826752.

5. Aristotle, *Metaphysics*, book IV, part 3.

6. Attributed to Avicenna in Andrew Razeghi, *The Riddle: Where Ideas Come From and How to Have Better Ones* (Jossey-Bass, 2008), 169.

7. Richard Dawkins, "Science Is Not an Instrument of Patriarchal Oppression," *The Spectator*, March 13, 2021, https://www.spectator.co.uk/article/science-is-not-an-instrument-of-patriarchal-oppression/.

8. Ludwig Wittgenstein, *Tractatus Logico-Philosophicus*, trans. F. P. Ramsey and C. K. Ogden, ed. Mark A. Joseph (Broadview Press, 2014), 6.52, (https://wittgensteinproject.org/w/index.php/Tractatus_Logico-Philosophicus_(English)#top).

9. Roger Ebert, "How I Believe in God," RogerEbert.com, 2012, https://www.rogerebert.com/roger-ebert/how-i-believe-in-god.

10. David Hume, *An Enquiry Concerning Human Understanding*, ed. Tom Beauchamp (Clarendon Press, 2000), 123.

11. A. J. Ayer, interviewed by Bryan Magee, 1976, *Men of Ideas*, https://www.youtube.com/watch?v=4cnRJGs08hE.

2. Can We Know Anything About God?

1. Alvin Plantinga, *Knowledge and Christian Belief* (Eerdmans, 2015), 3.

2. Plantinga, *Knowledge and Christian Belief*, 6.

3. Plantinga, *Knowledge and Christian Belief*, 6

4. G. W. F. Hegel, *Science of Logic* (Routledge, 1969), 134.

5. Wittgenstein, *Tractatus Logico-Philosophicus*, preface.

6. Jim McCrea, "Knowledge and Reality vs. Modern Philosophical Errors," *Truth in Philosophy*, last updated 2021, https://sites.google.com/site/truthinphilosophy/knowledge-and-reality-vs-modern-philosophical-errors?fbclid=IwAR1xp7OgEHfGbtDiXwPFW-jDffUIY2cQC72_6912eizfYai69yQrSE-TFAk.

3. Are All Things God?

1. William Shakespeare, *As You Like It*, 2.7.139. References are to act, scene, and line.

2. William Shakespeare, *Hamlet*, 5.2.10–11.

3. Justin Brierley, *The Surprising Rebirth of Belief in God: Why the New Atheism Grew Old and Secular Thinkers Are Considering Christianity Again* (Tyndale Elevate, 2023), 195–96.

4. Does Science Disprove God?

1. Julian Baggini, *Atheism: A Very Short Introduction* (Oxford University Press, 2003), 6.

5. Is God Too Good to Be True?

1. Jordan Peterson, *12 Rules for Life: An Antidote to Chaos* (Random House Canada, 2018), 196.

2. Jordan Peterson, "The Perfect Mode of Being | Jonathan Pageau," YouTube, March 1, 2021, https://www.youtube.com/watch?v=2rAqVmZwqZM&t=3291s.

3. C. S. Lewis, "Answers to Questions on Christianity," in *God in the Dock: Essays on Theology and Ethics*, ed. Walter Hooper (Eerdmans, 1970), 48.

4. C. S. Lewis, *Mere Christianity* (HarperCollins, 2001), 40.

5. H. Richard Niebuhr, *The Kingdom of God in America* (Wesleyan University Press, 1988), 193.

6. C. S. Lewis, "Bulverism," in *God in the Dock: Essays on Theology and Ethics*, ed. Walter Hooper (Eerdmans, 1970), 300–301.

7. Thomas Nagel, *The Last Word* (Oxford University Press, 1997), 130.

8. C. S. Lewis, *Mere Christianity* (HarperCollins, 2001), 27.

9. C. S. Lewis, *Miracles* (HarperCollins, 2001), 130.

10. Lewis, *Miracles*, 150.

11. C. S. Lewis, "Man or Rabbit," in *God in the Dock: Essays on Theology and Ethics*, ed. Walter Hooper (Eerdmans, 1970), 109.

6. *Is Religion the Opium of the People?*

1. Sigmund Freud, *Civilization and Its Discontents*, trans. Joan Riviere (Dover Publications, 1994), 9.

2. Karl Marx, *Critique of Hegel's "Philosophy of the Right,"* trans. Annette Jolin and Joseph O'Malley (Cambridge University Press, 1970), 131.

3. Peter Kreeft, *Socratic Logic: A Logic Text Using Socratic Method, Platonic Questions & Aristotelian Principles* (St. Augustine's Press, 2004), 81.

4. Antonin Scalia, "Prayer at Public Ceremonies," in *The Essential Scalia: The Constitution, the Courts, and the Rule of Law*, ed. Jeffrey Sutton and Edward Whelan (Crown Forum, 2020), 125.

5. Paul Vitz, "Freud's Unacknowledged Theory of Unbelief: Oedipal Atheism," in *Faith of the Fatherless: The Psychology of Atheism* (Ignatius Press, 2013).

6. Lewis, "Bulverism," in *God in the Dock*, ed. Hooper, 300.

7. Lewis, "Bulverism," 300.

8. Thomas Sowell, "It is amazing how many people think they can answer an argument," X, October 18, 2018, https://x.com/ThomasSowell/status/1052911555656990720.

7. Can Psychology Explain Away God?

1. Steven Pinker, "The Evolutionary Psychology of Religion," Freedom from Religion Foundation, 2004, https://ffrf.org/about/getting-acquainted/item/13184-the-evolutionary-psychology-of-religion.

2. Martin Seligman, *Authentic Happiness: Using the New Positive Psychology to Realize Your Potential for Lasting Fulfillment* (Simon and Schuster, 2002), 59.

3. Christopher Kaczor, *The Gospel of Happiness: How Secular Psychology Points to the Wisdom of Christian Practice*, 2nd ed. (St. Augustine's Press, 2019).

4. Stephen Cranney, "The Influence of Religiosity/Spirituality on Sex Life Satisfaction and Sexual Frequency: Insights from the Baylor Religion Survey," *Review of Religious Research* 62 (2020): 289–314.

5. Seligman, *Authentic Happiness*, 257.

6. Paul C. Vitz and Craig S. *Titus, A Catholic Christian Meta-Model of the Person: Integration with Psychology and Mental Health Practice* (Divine Mercy University, 2020).

7. René Girard, "Generative Scapegoating," in *Violent Origins: Walter Burkert, René Girard, and Jonathan Z. Smith on Ritual Killing and Cultural Formation*, ed. Robert G. Hamerton-Kelly (Stanford University Press, 1987), 122.

8. Noah J. Goldstein, Steve J. Martin, and Robert Cialdini, *Yes! 50 Scientifically Proven Ways to Be Persuasive* (New York: Free Press, 2009), vii.

9. David Masci and Gregory A. Smith, "7 Facts About American Catholics," https://www.pewresearch.org/fact-tank/2018/10/10/7-facts-about-american-catholics/.

10. There are approximately 70,412,021 Catholics in the United States, and Pew reports that 3.3 percent of them attend Mass more than once a week.

11. US Conference of Catholic Bishops, *The Catholic Church in America: Meeting Real Needs in Your Neighborhood* (Catholic Information Project, 2006).

8. Does Beauty Point to God?

1. Plato, *Phaedrus*, trans. Alexander Nehamas and Paul Woodruff, 250d.

2. Plato, *Symposium*, trans. Benjamin Jowett, 211a.

3. On this topic, see Jan Aertsen, *Medieval Philosophy and the Transcendentals: The Case of Thomas Aquinas* (Studien Und Texte Zur Geistesgeschichte Des Mittelalters) (Brill Academic Publishers, 1996).

4. Eleonore Stump, "Beauty as a Road to God," *Sacred Music* 134, no. 4 (2007): 13–14.

5. Stump, "Beauty as a Road to God," 15.

6. Stump, "Beauty as a Road to God," 15.

7. Stump, "Beauty as a Road to God," 16.

8. Stump, "Beauty as a Road to God," 17.

9. Stump, "Beauty as a Road to God," 24.

10. Stump, "Beauty as a Road to God," 24.

11. Stump, "Beauty as a Road to God," 24.

12. Stump, "Beauty as a Road to God," 26.

13. C. S. Lewis, *The Weight of Glory and Other Addresses* (HarperCollins, 2001), 30–31.

14. Stump, "Beauty as a Road to God," 14.

15. Joseph Ratzinger, *Salt of the Earth: Christianity and the Catholic Church at the End of the Millennium* (interview with Peter Seewald), trans. Adrian Walker (Ignatius Press, 1997), 32.

9. Are There Immaterial Realities?

1. Paul Davies, "Is Nature Mathematical?" *New Scientist*, March 21, 1992, https://www.newscientist.com/article/mg13318134-400-is-nature-mathematical/.

10. What Caused the Universe?

1. William Lane Craig, "The *Kalam* Cosmological Argument," Reasonable Faith with William Lane Craig, 2015, https://www.reasonablefaith.org/writings/popular-writings/existence-nature-of-god/the-kalam-cosmological-argument#:~:text=To%20claim%20that%20something%20can,past%20for%20no%20reason%20whatsoever.

2. Craig, "The *Kalam* Cosmological Argument."

11. What Is Causing the Universe to Continue to Exist?

1. *Summa Theologiae* I.2.3.

2. *Summa Theologiae* I.2.3.

3. Bertrand Russell, "Why I Am Not a Christian," Bertrand Russell Society Page, 1927, https://users.drew.edu/~jlenz/whynot.html.

12. Are Faith and Reason Opposed?

1. Richard Dawkins, *The God Delusion* (Mariner Books, 2008), 14.

2. See John Duns Scotus, *Treatise on the First Principle*, trans. Thomas M. Ward (Hackett, 2024).

3. Richard Dawkins, *The God Delusion* (First Mariner Books, 2008), 102.

4. Dawkins, *The God Delusion*, 101.

13. Can We Know What God Is Not?

1. Eleonore Stump, "Thomas Aquinas," *A Now You Know Study Guide* (2016), 29.

14. Are We All Atheists?

1. Richard Dawkins, "Militant Atheism," TED Conferences, February 2002, https://www.ted.com/talks/richard_dawkins_militant_atheism?subtitle=en.

2. Bill Vallicella, "Some of Us Just Go One God Further," Maverick Philosopher, July 26, 2010, https://maverickphilosopher.typepad.com/maverick_philosopher/2010/07/some-of-us-just-go-one-god-further.html.

3. David Hume, "The Sceptic," section 44; Q/drawing from Cicero, *Disputations* V.40.

4. William Lane Craig, "The Absurdity of Life Without God," Veritas Forum, 2011, https://www.reasonablefaith.org/videos/lectures/the-absurdity-of-life-without-god-veritas-forum-chicago.

5. Jean-Paul Sartre, *Existentialism and Human Emotions* (Kensington Publishing Corp., 1957), 23.

6. Geoffrey Miller, "So much weird cope in the replies to this simple point," X, January 5, 2023, https://x.com/primalpoly/status/1611036404800421891.

15. Are There Many Gods?

1. *Summa Contra Gentiles* I.42.3.

16. Is God like the Force in Star Wars?

1. *Summa Contra Gentiles* I.28.10. (https://isidore.co/aquinas/english/ContraGentiles1.htm#28).

2. *Summa Contra Gentiles* I.28.10.

3. *Summa Contra Gentiles* I.28.10.

4. *Summa Contra Gentiles* I.28.3.

5. *Summa Contra Gentiles* I.39.

6. *Summa Contra Gentiles* I.38.2.

17. Is God Intelligent?

1. John Stuart Mill, *Utilitarianism* (London, 1863), 14.

2. William Lane Craig, "Is Fine-Tuning Consistent with Theism?" The Good Book Blog, 2019, https://www.biola.edu/blogs/good-book-blog/2019/is-fine-tuning-consistent-with-theism1#:~:text=To%20say%20that%20the%20universe,to%20be%20well%2Destablished%20scientifically.

3. William Lane Craig, "What Is the Fine-Tuning Argument for the Existence of God?" Reasonable Faith with William Lane Craig, https://www.reasonablefaith.org/videos/interviews-panels/what-is-the-fine-tuning-argument-for-the-existence-of-god-bobby-conway.

4. Thomas Aquinas, *Summa Theologiae* I.14.5, reply 3.

5. *Summa Theologiae* I.14.3 corpus.

19. Can God Destroy Himself?

1. Anselm of Canterbury, *Proslogion*, trans. Sydney Norton Deane (Catholic Primer, 2005), 9.

2. Dawkins, *The God Delusion*, 101.

3. C. S. Lewis, *The Problem of Pain* (HarperCollins, 2001), 18.

4. Dawkins, *The God Delusion*, 101.

20. Is God Love?

1. Thomas Aquinas, *Summa Contra Gentiles* 1.91.

2. Greg Bottaro, *The Mindful Catholic: Finding God One Moment at a Time* (Wellspring, 2018), 60.

21. Why Isn't God's Existence Obvious?

1. *Jean-Paul Sartre: Basic Writings*, ed. Stephen Priest (Routledge, 2001), 34

2. A. J. Ayer, "What I Saw When I Was Dead," *The Sunday Telegraph*, August 28, 1988.

3. Peter Harrison, *Some New World: Myths of Supernatural Belief in a Secular Age* (Cambridge: Cambridge University Press, 2024), 363.

4. Daniel Simons, "The Monkey Business Illusion," YouTube, April 28, 2010, https://www.youtube.com/watch?v=IGQmdoK_ZfY.

5. Kevin Grove, "Why I Teach: Life, Sweetness, and Hope" (2024 Sheedy Address, Notre Dame, IN, December 3, 2024.

22. Can Evil Be a Means to the Good?

1. Epictetus, *Discourses and Enchiridion*, trans. Thomas W. Higginson (New York: Walter J. Black, Inc., 1944), 331.

2. Martha Washington to Mercy Otis Warren, December 26, 1789, https://marthawashington.us/items/show/25.html.

3. Aeschylus, *Agamemnon*, I.176, https://www.open.ac.uk/people/sites/www.open.ac.uk.people/files/files/aeschylus-agamemnon-definitive.pdf.

4. Léon Bloy, *The Pilgrim of the Absolute: A Selection of His Writings*, trans. John Coleman and Harry Lorin (Cluny Media, 2017), 251.

23. Does Any Evil Disprove God's Existence?

1. Attributed to Epictetus in David Hume, *Dialogues Concerning Natural Religion* (1779), 186.

2. Eleonore Stump, *Wandering in Darkness: Narrative and the Problem of Suffering* (Clarendon Press, 2010), 3–4.

3. Jeremy Bentham, "Supply without *Journal of Law and Economics* Burden," cited in H. L. A. Hart, "Bentham and the United States of America," 19, no. 3 (1976): 550.

4. Cormac McCarthy, *Suttree* (Random House, 1979), 188.

24. Does Pointless Evil Disprove God's Existence?

1. Justin McBrayer, "Skeptical Theism," *Internet Encyclopedia of Philosophy*, https://iep.utm.edu/skept-th/.

2. Elisabeth Elliot, *Through Gates of Splendor* (Hendrickson Publishers, 1957), 265.

3. Timothy Keller, "Just because you can't see or imagine a good reason," X, October 23, 2018, https://x.com/timkellernyc/status/1054808539888345089.

25. *Why Is There Evil?*

1. William Shakespeare, *Macbeth*, 4.3.5–7.

2. Stump, *Wandering in Darkness*, 11.

3. Stump, *Wandering in Darkness*, 13.

4. Stump, *Wandering in Darkness*, 27.

5. Paul Mankowski, letter to Rod Dreher, quoted in "The Life and Death of Paul Mankowski," *American Conservative*, September 10, 2020, https://www.theamericanconservative.com/life-and-death-of-paul-mankowski-sj/.

6. Stump, *Wandering in Darkness*, 375.

7. Stump, *Wandering in Darkness*, 455.

8. Fulton Sheen, *Through the Year with Fulton Sheen: Inspirational Readings for Each Day of the Year*, ed. Henry Dieterich (Ignatius, 2003), 58.

9. Walter J. Ciszek, *He Leadeth Me* (Image Books, 2014), 75.

26. *Does Jesus Reveal God?*

1. Timothy Keller, "Exclusivity: How Can There Be Just One True Religion?" Gospel in Life, YouTube, August 10, 2015, https://www.youtube.com/watch?v=75qetP4dRAA.

2. Timothy Keller, *The Reason for God: Belief in an Age of Skepticism* (Penguin, 2008), 9.

3. Keller, *The Reason for God*, 9.

28. *Is the Bible Meaningful?*

1. Jordan Peterson, *We Who Wrestle with God: Perceptions of the Divine* (Portfolio/Penguin, 2024), xxvii.

2. Alasdair MacIntyre, *After Virtue: A Study in Moral Theology* (University of Notre Dame Press, 2007), 216.

3. Cited in Cain, William E, "The Denial of Peter: René Girard, Mimetic Desire, and Conversion," *Contagion: Journal of Violence, Mimesis, and Culture* 29 (2022), 101.

4. Peterson, *We Who Wrestle with God*, 251.

5. Peterson, *We Who Wrestle with God*, 112.

6. Peterson, *We Who Wrestle with God*, 194.

7. Peterson, *We Who Wrestle with God*, 268.

8. Scott Hahn, *A Father Who Keeps His Promises: God's Covenant Love in Scripture* (Servant Books, 1998), 26.

9. Hahn, *A Father Who Keeps His Promises*, 26.

10. Peterson, *We Who Wrestle with God*, 272.

11. Joseph Henrich et al., "The Puzzle of Monogamous Marriage," *Philosophical Transactions of the Royal Society of London Series B* 367 (2012): 669, doi:10.1098/rstb.2011.0290.

29. *Is the Bible Deficient?*

1. Sam Harris, "Jordan Peterson & Sam Harris Try to Find Something They Agree On," YouTube, December 25, 2023, https://www.youtube.com/watch?v=2d3sk9gPfOA.

30. *Is the Bible Dogmatic?*

1. Harris, "Jordan Peterson & Sam Harris Try to Find Something They Agree On."

2. Harris, "Jordan Peterson & Sam Harris Try to Find Something They Agree On."

3. Harris, "Jordan Peterson & Sam Harris Try to Find Something They Agree On."

4. Peterson, "Jordan Peterson & Sam Harris Try to Find Something They Agree On."

5. Bernard Lonergan, *Method in Theology* (University of Toronto Press, 1971), 268.

6. Harris, "Jordan Peterson & Sam Harris Try to Find Something They Agree On."

7. Karl Keating, *Catholicism and Fundamentalism* (Ignatius Press, 1988), 126.

8. Plantinga, *Knowledge and Christian Belief*, 14.

9. Joseph Cardinal Ratzinger, "Crisis in Catechetics," *Canadian Catholic Review*, June 1983, 178.

31. Is the Bible True?

1. Jordan Peterson, interviewed by Brett McKay, "Exploring Archetypes with Jordan B. Peterson," The Art of Manliness, 2017, https://www.artofmanliness.com/character/advice/podcast-335-using-power-myths-live-flourishing-life/.

2. William Bruce Cameron, *Informal Sociology: A Casual Introduction to Sociological Thinking* (Random House, 1963), 13.

3. Jordan Peterson, "Biblical Series I: Introduction to the Idea of God," YouTube, May 20, 2017, https://www.youtube.com/watch?v=f-wWBGo6a2w&t=2727s.

4. Jordan Peterson, interviewed by Brett McKay, "Exploring Archetypes," Beyond Human Nature, December 6, 2017, https://beyondhumannature.wordpress.com/2017/12/06/exploring-archetypes-jordan-peterson-transcript/.

5. Jordan Peterson, interviewed by Joe Rogan, "Joe Rogan Experience #1070—Jordan Peterson," PowerfulJRE, YouTube, January 30, 2018, https://www.youtube.com/watch?v=6T7pUEZfgdI.

6. Jordan Peterson, "Dr. Jordan B. Peterson on Ideology, Logos & Belief Pt. 1," YouTube, April 11, 2021, https://www.youtube.com/watch?v=blf_AUBbbk8 (transcript, https://podscripts.co/podcasts/the-jordan-b-peterson-podcast/ideology-*logos*-belief).

7. C. S. Lewis, "Myth Became Fact," in *God in the Dock: Essays on Theology and Ethics*, ed. Walter Hooper (Eerdmans, 1970), 59.

8. Cited in Randy Boyagoda, "Cordially, Richard John Neuhaus," *First Things* (August 2012): 18.

Christopher Kaczor is the Honorary Professor for the Renewal of Catholic Intellectual Life at Bishop Barron's Word on Fire Institute, a professor of philosophy at Loyola Marymount University, and a visiting fellow at the University of Notre Dame.

Kaczor graduated from the Honors Program at Boston College and earned a doctorate in philosophy from the University of Notre Dame. A Fulbright Scholar, he completed postdoctoral work as an Alexander von Humboldt Foundation German Chancellor Fellow at the University of Cologne. He was appointed a corresponding member of Vatican City's Pontifical Academy for Life, a fellow of the Center for Christian Thought at Biola University, and a William E. Simon Visiting Fellow in the James Madison Program at Princeton University.

Kaczor, the winner of a John Templeton Foundation grant, has published more than 120 scholarly articles and book chapters. An award-winning author of seventeen books, Kaczor has been featured in *The New York Times*, *The Washington Post*, *The Wall Street Journal*, *Los Angeles Times*, *HuffPost*, and *National Review*, and on NPR, BBC, EWTN, ABC, NBC, FOX, CBS, MSNBC, TEDx, *The Today Show*, and *The Jordan B. Peterson Podcast*.

Kaczor lives with his wife in Los Angeles, California.

Website: faculty.lmu.edu/ckaczor
Facebook: christopher.kaczor
X: Prof_Kaczor

Bishop Robert Barron, head of the Diocese of Winona–Rochester, is the founder of Word on Fire Catholic Ministries.

Founded in 1865, Ave Maria Press, a ministry of the Congregation of Holy Cross, is a Catholic publishing company that serves the spiritual and formative needs of the Church and its schools, institutions, and ministers; Christian individuals and families; and others seeking spiritual nourishment.

For a complete listing of titles from

Ave Maria Press

Sorin Books

Forest of Peace

Christian Classics

visit www.avemariapress.com